The well-being of youth in China is a critical issue for the future of China and the world. Despite the miraculous rise of the Chinese economy, most children from rural backgrounds are still raised in a very challenging environment, and their human capital is not sufficiently developed. This book provides a comprehensive analysis of this issue and will likely have a huge impact for policy consideration.

James Jianzhang Liang, Co-founder and Chairman of Ctrip

Child and Youth Well-being in China

The true measure of any society is how it treats its children, who are in turn that society's future. Making use of data from the longitudinal Chinese Family Panel Studies survey, the authors of this timely study provide a multi-faceted description and analysis of China's younger generations. They assess the economic, physical, and social-emotional well-being as well as the cognitive performance and educational attainment of China's children and youth. They pay special attention to the significance of family and community contexts, including the impact of parental absence on millions of left-behind children.

Throughout the volume, the authors delineate various forms of disparities, especially the structural inequalities maintained by the Chinese Party-state and the vulnerabilities of children and youth in fragile families and communities. They also analyze the social attitudes and values of Chinese youth. Having grown up in a period of sustained prosperity and greater individual choice, the younger Chinese cohorts are more independent in spirit, more open-minded socially, and significantly less deferential to authority than older cohorts.

There is growing recognition in China of the importance of investing in children's future and of helping the less advantaged. Substantial improvements in child and youth well-being have been achieved in a time of growing economic prosperity. Strong political commitment is needed to sustain existing efforts and to overcome the many obstacles that remain. This book will be of considerable interest to researchers of Chinese society and development.

Lijun Chen, Senior Researcher, Chapin Hall at the University of Chicago, USA.

Qiang Ren, Associate Professor of Sociology, Co-PI of CFPS, Peking University, China.

Dali L. Yang, William C. Reavis Professor of Political Science and the College, the University of Chicago, USA.

Di Zhou, Ph.D. student, Department of Sociology, New York University, USA.

Routledge Research on Asian Development

Development and Gender Capital in India
Change, Continuity and Conflict in Kerala
Shoba Arun

Bangladesh's Graduation from the Least Developed Countries Group
Pitfalls and Promises
Edited by Debapriya Bhattacharya

Regional Cooperation for Peace and Development
Japan and South Korea in Southeast Asia
Edited by Brendan Howe

Child and Youth Well-being in China
Lijun Chen, Dali L. Yang, Di Zhou, and Qiang Ren

Child and Youth Well-being in China

Lijun Chen, Dali L. Yang,
Di Zhou, and Qiang Ren

LONDON AND NEW YORK

First published 2019
by Routledge
2 Park Square, Milton Park, Abingdon, Oxon OX14 4RN

and by Routledge
52 Vanderbilt Avenue, New York, NY 10017

First issued in paperback 2020

Routledge is an imprint of the Taylor & Francis Group, an informa business

© 2019 Lijun Chen, Dali L. Yang, Di Zhou, and Qiang Ren

The right of Lijun Chen, Dali L. Yang, Di Zhou, and Qiang Ren to be identified as authors of this work has been asserted by them in accordance with sections 77 and 78 of the Copyright, Designs and Patents Act 1988.

All rights reserved. No part of this book may be reprinted or reproduced or utilised in any form or by any electronic, mechanical, or other means, now known or hereafter invented, including photocopying and recording, or in any information storage or retrieval system, without permission in writing from the publishers.

Trademark notice: Product or corporate names may be trademarks or registered trademarks, and are used only for identification and explanation without intent to infringe.

British Library Cataloguing-in-Publication Data
A catalogue record for this book is available from the British Library

Library of Congress Cataloging-in-Publication Data
A catalog record has been requested for this book

ISBN 13: 978-0-367-67036-8 (pbk)
ISBN 13: 978-0-367-08613-8 (hbk)

Typeset in Times New Roman
by Out of House Publishing

Contents

List of figures viii
List of tables ix
Acknowledgments xii

1 Introduction 1

2 The institutional and policy context 14

3 Economic well-being 26

4 Physical well-being 33

5 Psychological and social well-being 41

6 Cognitive development and educational attainments 49

7 Community and family 63

8 Youth values and attitudes 77

9 Migration and parental absence for left-behind children 90

10 Parental absence and child development outcomes 101

11 Conclusion 120

Bibliography 131
Index 154

List of figures

2.1	Rural vs. urban population in China, 1996–2015	16
2.2	China's population pyramids 1990, 2000, 2010, 2020	20
2.3	Number of primary schools in China, 1999–2016	21
2.4	Primary school class size in China, 1999–2013	23
3.1	Children's family economic conditions, 2014	29
5.1	Selected variables on psychological and social well-being of children, 2014	43
6.1	School enrollment ratios in China, 1990–2016	50
6.2	Educational status of youth aged 16–19 by living arrangement (%), 2014	60
7.1	Attitudes on parental responsibility in rural and urban China, 2014	74
8.1	Deference to parental authority among the 1990s cohort	79
8.2	"Children should give up their own will to realize parents' wishes"	80
8.3	Woman's gender role, by cohort	81
8.4	"One needs to have at least one son to carry on the family lineage"	82
8.5	Men should prioritize career; women should prioritize family, the 1990s cohort	83
8.6	"What would make a child successful in the future?", age 12 to 30	84
8.7	Evaluation of government performance by community type, 1990s cohort	87
9.1	Child living arrangements by child age in 2010	95
9.2	Months children had father at home in 2014 by child age	96
9.3	Months child had mother at home in 2014 by child age	96
10.1	Average happiness score by living arrangement and community type	108

List of tables

1.1	Characteristics of children in rural and urban communities in China in the 2010 Baseline Survey	7
1.2	Criteria for grouping of children into six living arrangement types	8
1.3	Attributes of children in different living arrangements in 2010	10
3.1	Children's family economic conditions by community type, 2014	27
3.2	Changes in children's family economic conditions, 2010 to 2014	28
3.3	Children's family economic conditions by living arrangement, 2014	29
3.4	Changes in children's family economic conditions by living arrangement, 2010 to 2014	31
4.1	Children's health conditions by community type, 2014	34
4.2	Changes in children's health conditions, 2010 to 2014	36
4.3	Children's health conditions by living arrangement, 2014	37
4.4	Changes in children's health conditions by living arrangement, 2010 to 2014	38
5.1	Social-emotional well-being by gender in 2014	44
5.2	Children's psychological and social well-being by family structure (%), 2010	46
5.3	Children's psychological and social well-being by family structure (%), 2014	46
5.4	Self-esteem and self-efficacy for children in various living arrangements in 2010 and 2014	47
6.1.1	School enrollment and college aspirations (%), 2014	51
6.1.2	Changes in school enrollment and college aspirations (percentage points), 2010 to 2014	51

x List of tables

6.2.1	School enrollment and college aspirations by living arrangement (%), 2014	52
6.2.2	School enrollment and college aspirations by living arrangement (%), 2010	52
6.3	Reported class size in rural and urban areas (age 10–15), 2014	54
6.4	Study engagement, school satisfaction and self-reported performance for children aged 10–15, 2010 to 2014	55
6.5.1	Children's test scores, 2014	57
6.5.2	Changes in children's test score (age 10–15), 2010 to 2014	57
6.6	Children's test scores by living arrangement (age 10–15), 2010 and 2014	58
6.7	Education status of 16–19 year olds by community type (%), 2014	60
7.1	Children's community conditions by community type, 2010 to 2014	65
7.2	Family relations with neighbors and relatives, 2014	66
7.3	Observed home environment by living arrangement (age 0–15), 2010 to 2014	68
7.4	Caregiver involvement in child education in China, 2010 and 2014	69
7.5	Caregiver involvement in child education by living arrangement, 2010 and 2014	70
7.6.1	Positive parenting factor scores by community type (ages 10–15), 2014	72
7.6.2	Positive parenting factor scores by living arrangement (ages 10–15), 2014	72
8.1	What would make a child successful in the future (%), by cohort	85
9.1	Characteristics of children in different living situations in China	92
9.2	Local or inter-provincial migration patterns of parents of left-behind children	93
9.3	Inter-regional migration patterns of parents of left-behind children	94
9.4	Months children had father or mother at home in 2014 by region (%)	97
9.5	Characteristics of primary caregivers of all children by living arrangements (%)	99
10.1	Percentage of children sick last month by parental absence in rural/urban communities (2010–2014)	104

10.2	Random-effects logistic regression for probability of sickness for children in rural and urban communities	106
10.3	Random effects GLS regression estimates of happiness of children and youth in China in 2010, 2012, 2014	110
10.4	Linear regression with cluster robust estimates for vocabulary test scores of children and youth in China in 2010 and 2014	113
10.5	Linear regression with cluster robust estimates for math test scores of children and youth in China in 2010 and 2014	115
11.1	Pre-school education development goals	126

Acknowledgments

In researching and writing this book, we have incurred many debts. The analysis is based on survey data from the China Family Panel Studies (CFPS), a project that was launched in 2010 by the Institute of Social Science Survey (ISSS) of Peking University. We are thus deeply grateful to the CFPS leadership, led by Yu Xie, Xiaobo Zhang, Ping Tu, and Qiang Ren, and the hundreds of participants who carried out the survey.

This book draws on data from the 2010, 2012, and 2014 waves of the CFPS. It builds on a previous report by three of the authors (Chen, Yang, and Ren) on the state of the children in China (Chapin Hall at the University of Chicago, 2015). That report, drawing on the CFPS baseline survey of 2010, was also published in Chinese by the Social Sciences Academic Press in China. We remain indebted to all who helped make that report possible. While retaining key themes from the 2015 report, we have in this book updated and significantly expanded the coverage as well as added chapters on the impact of parental absence and on youth values and attitudes. We were fortunate to have Di Zhou join the project for the 2017–2018 academic year. She worked with Chen and Yang to draft newer sections of the text and played an indispensable role in helping to coordinate the entire project. We very much appreciate her contributions and are pleased to have her join us as a co-author.

We are especially grateful to Fred Wulczyn, senior research fellow at Chapin Hall, for his guidance and advice throughout the project. Professor James Heckman and the Center for the Economics of Human Development he directs have been a source of intellectual inspiration and nurturance. We have also received helpful comments and encouragement from Zhixin Du, Danhua Lin, Xi Song, and Ming Wen, among others.

Several University of Chicago students provided able research assistance at different stages of this project and deserve a special note of thanks. Yinxian Zhang and Yuanqi Wang worked with us on the

2015 report. Zhenying Tian, Yanhan Fang, Steven Ren, and Zhichen Sha helped us wrestle with the CFPS datasets and the vast literature on child development and attended to various details. All but Yinxian were interns of the Jeff Metcalf Internship Program of the College of the University of Chicago. Dali Yang wishes to thank the Metcalf Program administrators and the College for their support. He also acknowledges support from the Social Sciences Divisional Research Fund.

The seeds for this project were planted when a series of workshops and symposia were convened on social survey collaboration at the University of Chicago Center in Beijing, where Yang was faculty director. He is grateful to the Ford Foundation for its grant to support the initial symposium and to the Center team, then led by Beth Bader and joined by Ji Yuan and later Xueming Liang, for their superb support for that and subsequent workshops. Lijun Chen and Dali Yang were then awarded a grant from the Joint Research Fund (Award No. 2014–003 "State of the Child in China"), established by Chapin Hall and the University of Chicago to support collaborative research between the two institutions. We also gratefully acknowledge the financial support from the University of Chicago Center in Beijing for a seminar in June 2018 in which we presented our findings to and learned from a group of child development researchers and practitioners.

Last but certainly not least, we thank Helena Hurd, Development Studies editor of Routledge, for her encouragement and thoughtful suggestions and the comments of the reviewers. Matthew Shobbrook of Routledge and Ruth-Anne Hurst at Out of House Publishing ably shepherded us through the editorial and production process. Lingnan He and Zhaodi Chen compiled the index.

1 Introduction

Significance of the study

Protecting and promoting the well-being of children, as stipulated in the United Nations Convention on the Rights of the Child (CRC), has been the obligation of member countries. As an early signatory to the CRC, the People's Republic of China (hereafter, "China") has formulated ambitious ten-year programs for the development of children since early 1990s. Whereas through the 2000s China stood out for its controversial and draconian birth planning policies and practices, the national sentiment about children has shifted rapidly in the 2010s. In the most recent child development program, the China National Program for Child Development (2011–2020), children are recognized as major resources for sustainable social and economic development of the country (State Council 2011b).[1] Promoting child development is now given strategic importance, especially in terms of improving the "quality" of the Chinese people and building up the national human capital. The program spells out clear aims for child development in five areas: health care, education, welfare, social environment, and legal protection.

Although China has made great achievement in promoting child development and protecting children's rights in the past three decades, many challenges remain, including regional gaps in child development level, children in poverty, institutional barriers to equal access to quality education, and public health hazards. Building on our earlier work (Chen, Yang, and Ren 2015) and making use of more recent longitudinal data from a nationally representative household survey (Xie and Hu 2014), this study aims to provide a comprehensive understanding of the status of child development in China. Through detailed description and analysis of child development in major domains, our study documents the progress that has been made, specifies the areas that need to be improved, and identifies the vulnerable children that are at risk and need social services. Many readers will likely be quite interested to see the major changes in child development in the first half of the 2010s and ponder their connections with and implications for various government initiatives.

As of the last national Population Census in 2010, China was home to 227.2 million children aged 0–14, which accounted for 16.5 percent of the total population in Mainland China (National Bureau of Statistics [NBS] 2016). Since the 1980s, the living conditions and environments of Chinese children have changed dramatically due to rapid industrialization, massive urbanization, and the enforcement of a stringent family planning policy (World Bank 2015). On the one hand, with rapid economic development, the economic conditions and physical well-being of Chinese children have generally improved, including during the time period our dataset covers. This is especially true for children in rural areas where tens of millions of parents now earn income from jobs in industry and services rather than in agriculture (NBS et al. 2017). On the other hand, China's stringent family planning policy, which officially allowed one child for each urban couple and at most two for a rural couple until the shift to a national two-children per couple policy in 2015, coupled with the effects of modernization has led to small family sizes throughout the country. As is well known, families have treated their only children like "little emperors", investing heavily in their education and overall well-being as well as placing enormous pressure on the children to perform in school tests, among others (Fong 2002; Rosenzweig and Zhang 2009a).

Yet the unbalanced economic growth in recent decades has also posed serious challenges for the (relative) well-being of children, especially those in the rural areas of less-developed regions within China. Four challenges stand out. First, economic disparities between rural and urban areas have remained and have even increased in certain dimensions during this period. While we recognize the shifting boundary between urban and rural, it is nonetheless striking that the urban per capita disposable income has been nearly three times the rural per capita net income (NBS 2015). In 2012, 128 million people, mostly rural residents, were still living in poverty with an annual per capita income of less than 2,300 Yuan (then about 1.6 USD per day) (China Academy of Sciences 2012). The income gaps between urban and rural areas both contribute to and are a consequence of the persistent rural-urban disparities in health and nutrition, child care and education, and other critical resources available to children.

Second, multiple researchers have identified various developmental deficits for migrant children (Wang and Zou 2010). As of 2015, 12.6 percent of the children population in China, about 34.3 million, were migrant children (NBS et al. 2017).[2] Generally speaking, the children of migrant workers have difficulty attending local public schools and gaining access to other public services because many municipalities have adopted exclusionary policies and practices against migrant laborers (Chan 2009). Even if these children were given access, they would normally be at a disadvantage in comparison to their urban counterparts as most migrant workers earn a relatively meager income and tend to have to cope with poor living conditions, housing instability, and job insecurity.

Third, in response to the high costs and exclusionary policies imposed in urban areas, many migrant workers with children had little choice but to leave their children behind in their rural hometowns. In 2015, about one quarter of all children in China (25.4 percent), or a whopping 68.8 million, were left behind in either rural or urban areas (NBS et al. 2017).[3] Previous research shows long periods of parental absence may adversely affect the psychological, social, and cognitive development of children, leading to problems such as low self-esteem, depression, and lack of motivation at school, among others (Wen and Lin 2012; Xiang 2007). Without proper adult supervision, left-behind children are also more likely to be victimized (Chen et al. 2009).

Fourth, a variety of government policies and practices – particularly the consolidation of rural schools in the first decade of this century – have exacerbated the plight of many rural children even while these policies were intended to improve the quality of education, among others. The school consolidation policy, for example, is believed to have made it more difficult for some children living in remote areas to gain access to education and to have contributed to classroom overcrowding (Zhao and Parolin 2011).

Many organizations and scholars, both in China and abroad, have conducted academic studies and research on the socioeconomic conditions of children in China and their developmental outcomes. The poor conditions of vulnerable children, especially rural left-behind children and migrant children, have especially received significant media coverage in China and have become a growing concern for the Chinese government and the general public. These studies and reports have generated numerous recommendations for addressing the developmental disparities between rural and urban areas and improve the well-being of children (All-China Women's Federation 2013; New Citizen Program 2014; Xiang 2007; Zou, Qu, and Zhang 2005).

Because of limitations in the availability of data, existing studies of child development in China tend to be focused on a limited number of child development outcomes. This is also the case with official documents. For instance, in terms of child well-being, official government reports tend to focus on indicators such as infant mortality, physical health, and school enrollment, while social-emotional well-being indicators and other subjective well-being indicators – such as self-esteem and sense of happiness – are largely absent (e.g., NBS et al. 2017; NHFPC 2015). Moreover, most studies on child well-being are based on samples drawn from a few regions and certain age groups. Therefore, their findings cannot be generalized to the whole child population at the national level.

Based on findings from our analysis of longitudinal household survey data that are nationally representative, our study strives to offer a comprehensive view of the conditions of China's children and youth. It covers all major domains of child development, including children's physical health, mental and psychological well-being, economic and social well-being, their cognitive and educational performance, the influence of parenting practices, and, for youth, their social and political attitudes. We pay special attention to describing and dissecting the developmental disparities between children of rural and urban regions and between children with different living arrangements (for instance, between left-behind children with both parents absent, or one parent absent, and migrant children). We also strive to reveal variations in the ecological contexts of these children (i.e., the different conditions of their families and communities that may have contributed to their different developmental trajectories). We hope our analyses will help identify the most vulnerable groups of children in China and their developmental deficits. We also seek to illuminate the risks and protective factors in these children's social contexts and thus help government agencies and other stakeholders to formulate and implement targeted policies and programs to promote child well-being.

Multiple contexts of child well-being

Scientific research in child development has long recognized the importance of living environments and nurturing relationships for the healthy development of children and adolescents (Bronfenbrenner 1979; Phillips and Shonkoff 2000). Childhood experiences in multiple contexts—such as families, peer groups, schools, and communities—exert profound effects on children's development and well-being.

Typically, children spend most of their infancy and toddlerhood with parents and other caregivers at home. Family structure and functioning, spousal relationship, and parenting styles are all major factors affecting child development. Aside from socioeconomic resources of the family, a cognitively stimulating home environment and a nurturing caregiver-child relationship are essential to children's social and cognitive development (Conger, Conger, and Martin 2010). Childcare institutions, kindergartens, and schools are also major venues where children learn important social and emotional skills as well as academic knowledge (Durlak et al. 2011; Reynolds et al. 2011). Teaching quality and more generally school resources are major facilitators of student attainment of skills essential for students to become constructive members of society when they grow up (Lai, Sadoulet, and De Janvry 2011). The other major social context in which children learn to interact and prosper is the community. Community ecology such as social norms, neighborhood safety and poverty level, social support networks, availability of and access to social service facilities are all important to the well-being of children and their caregivers alike (Sampson 2003).

Given the close relationship between various ecological contexts and child well-being, children of lower socioeconomic status often face multiple disadvantages in both their families and communities. The unfavorable environments these vulnerable children find themselves in for no fault of their own will tend to have an adverse impact not only on the short-term development and long-term well-being of these children but also the development and well-being of the society they are part of. Therefore, this study aims to delineate the various social contexts, such as family functioning and community quality, that contribute to the developmental deficits of vulnerable children in China. We pay special attention to the rural-urban disparities in child well-being, particularly the developmental deficits of left-behind and migrant children. We also examine the family and social contexts of the children, especially parental absence, to highlight various factors that may have contributed to the rural-urban disparities of child well-being.

The China Family Panel Studies survey and data overview

This study is based on data from the 2010 baseline wave and 2014 wave of the China Family Panel Studies (CFPS) survey.[4] Designed and administered by Peking University, CFPS is a longitudinal survey of a nationally representative sample of nearly 15,000 families.[5] It adopts a stratified three-stage cluster sample design where over 600 urban and rural communities are selected for inclusion. From each community, 25 households are chosen at random (Xie and Hu 2014; Xie, Qiu, and Lu 2012). Data are collected for all sample communities and all members of sample households, including family members who are migrant workers.

The 2010 CFPS has data for 8,990 children between the ages of 0 and 15 years old, including caregiver reports for all children and direct interviews with children between 10 and 15 years old. The 2014 CFPS has data for 8,312 children aged 0–15. As a family panel survey, the 2014 data includes children from the baseline survey as well as children newly born into the original families and new families formed by original family members. Information collected in each wave includes outcomes on major domains of child well-being such as physical health, social-emotional development, cognitive development, and educational achievement. Key contextual information includes family living conditions, poverty level, parent education and employment, parenting behavior, and community contexts. In addition, both waves incorporated questions of social values and attitudes and political behaviors for the youth and adult population. The wealth of information on children and youth provides us with the opportunity to seek a comprehensive understanding of the development and well-being of children and youth in China.

Due to the complex sampling design and oversampling of children in some strata, the 2010 and 2014 CFPS data introduce population weights to account for sampling design, non-response, and post-stratification adjustment (Xie, Qiu, and Lu 2012). In conducting our analyses, we use the survey data analysis methods that take into account the survey design effect and unequal population weights. We used STATA in conducting the analysis and applied the STATA survey data analysis commands (Stata Corp 2013). We conducted analyses to examine child well-being outcomes in different social and familial contexts, with emphasis on changes between 2010 and 2014. Table 1.1 presents an overview of the characteristics of children included in this study from the 2010 CFPS baseline survey. Since the urban-rural disparity in child well-being is a major focus of our study, we present the basic demographic information of the sampled children by urban and rural community. We classify the children as rural or urban based on whether the sampled communities they live in are reported by the community administrator as a Villager's Committee (*Cun weihui* 村委会) or Urban Resident Committee (*Jü weihui* 居委会).

As shown in Table 1.1, 27 percent of the sampled children are living in urban communities. Our estimate of the urban child population is conservative compared to the Census estimate of the National Bureau

Table 1.1 Characteristics of children in rural and urban communities in China in the 2010 Baseline Survey

Characteristics	Rural (village)		Urban neighborhood		Total	
	N	%	N	%	N	%
All children	6,795	73.1	2,195	26.9	8,990	100.0
Child age						
0 to 5	2,526	37.0	817	34.1	3,343	36.2
6 to 10	2,068	31.2	681	31.8	2,749	31.4
11 to 15	2,201	31.8	697	34.1	2,898	32.4
Gender						
Female	3,189	45.1	1,049	47.4	4,238	45.7
Male	3,606	54.9	1,146	52.6	4,752	54.3
Ethnicity*						
Ethnic minority	920	18.8	178	9.3	1,098	16.3
Han ethnicity	5,875	81.2	2,017	90.7	7,892	84.7
Hukou registration*						
Urban hukou	567	7.5	1,525	69.0	2,092	24.0
Rural hukou	6,211	92.5	662	31.0	6,873	76.0
Location of hukou*						
In local county	6,488	96.0	1,826	84.0	8,314	92.8
In other county	173	2.5	243	11.1	416	4.8
In other province	117	1.5	118	5.0	235	2.4
# of Parents at Home*						
None	1,001	15.0	174	7.9	1,175	13.1
1 parent	1,126	15.5	268	12.7	1,394	14.8
2 parents	4,668	69.5	1,753	79.4	6,421	72.1
Region*						
Eastern	2,400	36.9	992	35.4	2,292	36.5
Central	2,017	31.6	800	43.3	2,817	34.7
Western	2,378	31.6	403	21.3	2,781	28.8

Note: 2010 CFPS child sample $N=8,990$. Percentages are weighted; counts are unweighted.
* $p < .05$ based on design-based Pearson chi-square statistic.

of Statistics (NBS), which identifies half of the Chinese population as urban based on physical residence (NBS 2010). Our estimate is more in line with the residence registration (*hukou*) status of the children. As we will explain in the next section, rural or urban community type and the *hukou* status of its residents are major institutional features that contribute to the urban-rural disparities in child well-being. Hence, we

Child living arrangements and parental absence

Given our concern with urban-rural disparities in child well-being, we are interested in better understanding the development of children who have experienced deprivation of parental care because their parents have sought economic opportunities as migrant workers. The massive internal migration is a bitter-sweet component of China's rapid economic ascent.

Table 1.1 shows that 13 percent of children live without parents at home, and another 15 percent have only one parent at home. A much higher proportion of rural children has no parents at home than urban children (15 percent vs. 8 percent). As we will discuss later, in contrast with the situation in the US, divorce, death, or out-of-wedlock birth account for only a small percentage of children's parental absence in China. The main driving force behind parental absence is the migration of parents in search of jobs. There are 7.2 percent of children whose *hukou* are not registered in the county or district they now reside, indicating that they migrated with their parents. However, most rural children whose father and/or mother migrate to (mostly) urban areas for jobs are left behind in their rural homes.

To better examine the development outcomes of children in different living arrangements, we have identified six family configurations based on four factors, parents' marriage status, child's hukou status, parental absence, and community type (urban vs. rural) (Table 1.2). For those

Table 1.2 Criteria for grouping of children into six living arrangement types

Child living arrangement	Parents alive & married/ cohabit	Local hukou	Parents live at home?	Community
Rural intact family	Yes	Yes	Both parents	Rural
Urban intact family	Yes	Yes	Both parents	Urban
Left-behind children— no parent	Yes	Yes	No parent at home	–
Left-behind children— one parent	Yes	Yes	One parent at home	–
Migrant children	Yes	No	–	–
Single parent/orphaned	No (Parents are divorced, dead, or unknown)			–

children whose parents are married or are cohabiting, we define those children whose registered *hukou* is not in the local county or city district as "migrant children". Table 1.3 shows that most migrant children live in coastal urban areas, but has rural *hukou*.[6] These are mostly rural children who migrated with their parents to urban areas in the coastal region who are kept from obtaining urban residence status in their current locales.[7] As we have pointed out, migrant children's lack of access to social services such as health care and public education in the host cities makes them vulnerable to developmental problems.

In contrast to the migrant children, those children with local *hukou* and both parents (married or cohabiting), are categorized into two groups based on whether both parents are present at home. Children who have both parents at home in either urban or rural communities are referred to as "intact families" for convenience, though we recognize the complexity of such a label. Left-behind children have one or both parents living away from home.

We put into a separate category those children who have a single parent or who have no surviving parents (orphaned). The reason for having a single parent may be for a variety of reasons, including separation, divorce, and death or disappearance of one of the parents, being different from left-behind children with one parent at home and the other away from home. While this category accounts for a small proportion of the sample, it nonetheless demands attention because these children tend to go through traumatic changes in their family circumstances that, especially in the Chinese context, may have severe consequences for child development.

We further differentiate the more broadly defined "left-behind children" into two: those with no parent at home and those with only one parent (father or mother) at home.[8] Whereas previously scholars and policymakers tended to use the broad definition of "left-behind children," in recent years the Chinese government has tended to refer only to the first group, children with both parents away from home, as being "left behind" (State Council 2016b). In this study we have chosen to include both broad and narrow definitions of "left-behind children" when warranted so as to compare the development and well-being between those with no parental guardianship at all and those with one parent who can still effectively exercise parental guardianship. As we will show in later chapters, the deprivation of parental care for left-behind children with no parent at home (narrow definition) has a significant impact on child development.

We have thus far provided an overview of the profile of China's children and youth from the CFPS 2010 and some of the key categories we

Table 1.3 Attributes of children in different living arrangements in 2010

Attributes	Rural intact	Urban intact	LBC—no parent	LBC—1 parent	Migrant children	Single-parent/orphan	Total
All children	4,494	1,463	920	1,114	622	377	8,990
Community type:							
Rural	4,494		804	955	277	265	6,795
Urban		1,463	116	159	345	112	2,195
Rural/Urban hukou							
Not rural hukou	367	1,089	111	151	270	104	2,092
Rural hukou	4,117	368	807	961	351	269	6,873
Local hukou							
Local hukou	4,494	1,463	920	1,114		345	8,336
Hukou outside county					397	21	418
Hukou outside province					225	11	236
Number of parents at home							
No parent			920			161	1,175
Only mother				932	56	95	1,083
Only father				182	8	121	311
Both parents	4,494	1,463			464		6,421
Age of child							
0 to 5	1,571	523	419	476	277	77	3,343
6 to 10	1,350	467	293	309	200	130	2,749
11 to 15	1,573	473	208	329	145	170	2,898

Mother's marriage status							
Married	4,488	1,463	916	1,108	622	47	8,644
Divorced, widowed, death	6		4	6		330	346
Father's marriage status							
Married	4,488	1,463	917	1,108	622	19	8,617
Divorced, widowed, death	6		3	6		358	373
Region							
Eastern	1,660	664	223	389	324	132	3,392
Central	1,239	548	378	332	193	127	2,817
Western	1,595	251	319	393	105	118	2,781

Note: Frequencies are unweighted. Parents of some children are reported to be divorced but they still live together.

have adopted for this study. In the rest of the volume, we will make use of the baseline data to make comparisons with data from CFPS 2014. Even though these two waves of the CFPS are only four years apart, we think our readers will be as impressed as we are with the speed of change concerning Chinese children and youth in this relatively brief period, encompassing the last years of the Hu Jintao and Wen Jiabao Administration and the first two years of the Xi Jinping Era.

We next provide a general overview of the institutional environment and policy context for the development and well-being of children and youth in China. We describe the *hukou* system, the urbanization process, the family planning policy, and school consolidation, and discuss their implications for child well-being. We then address different domains of child well-being outcomes in rural and urban areas and across six types of family arrangements in a series of short chapters:

3. Economic well-being: family poverty level and living conditions;
4. Children's physical health, including incidences of low birthweight, sickness and hospitalization, and obesity;
5. Psychological and social well-being, including sense of happiness, depression, self-esteem, and social skills;
6. Cognitive development and educational attainments, including school attendance and performance, vocabulary and math test scores, and school satisfaction.

In the rest of the volume, Chapter 7 examines the family and community contexts of children, including family structure, parenting behavior, and community resources. Chapter 8 looks at the civic culture of China's younger generation, with attention to youth attitudes toward authority, gender, and civic participation. Last but not least, we devote Chapters 9 and 10 to the consequences of migration and left-behind children. We first describe the patterns of migration and parental absence in Chinese families and then analyze the relationship between parental absence and child development. Finally, we summarize our findings in the concluding chapter and, to help anchor the findings in their historical context, also briefly review the major policies and initiatives launched after the time period covered in this book.

Notes

1 Heckman shows that investing in the early development of children has a much greater positive economic and social influence than later interventions (Heckman 2012).

2 Migrant children are individuals aged from 0 to 17 and whose place of residence is different from their household registration (*hukou*) for over six months. The statistics given by UNICEF excludes those whose current residential place is different from their household registration but within the same city-level administration (NBS et al., 2017).
3 Left-behind children, as defined by NBS et al. (2017), are children who "live in their original domicile, but do not live together with their parents, as either one parent or both parents have migrated". The distinction of rural left-behind children and urban left-behind children are made according to the family's household registration areas (NBS et al. 2017).
4 The 2012 wave of CFPS data is also included in our analysis in one chapter of the study.
5 Six provincial units, Hainan, Inner Mongolia, Ningxia, Qinghai, Xinjiang, and Tibet, are not included in the sample for various reasons. Four of them are ethnic autonomous regions located in remote areas and Hainan is a small island province. Together they make up about 5 percent of the total population in China.
6 In this study, we adopt a macro-regional classification scheme and have the following provincial units in each region in the CFPS datasets: the eastern region consists of Beijing plus the coastal provincial units of Tianjin, Hebei, Liaoning, Shanghai, Jiangsu, Zhejiang, Fujian, Shandong, Guangdong, and Guangxi; the central region includes Henan, Anhui, Jiangxi, Hunan, Hubei, Shanxi, Heilongjiang, and Jilin; the western region includes Chongqing, Sichuan, Guizhou, Yunnan, Shaanxi, and Gansu.
7 As the *hukou* system has been reformed, many small cities and towns have abolished the *hukou* restrictions for rural migrant families. However, the migrant children identified here do not include local migration from rural villages to urban areas in the same county or city-level administration.
8 Since only a minority of the left-behind children have only a father at home, we do not differentiate children with only a mother or father at home in most of our analysis.

2 The institutional and policy context

While child development and well-being are universal concerns, societies across time and space have adopted different institutional arrangements for them. These institutional arrangements constitute the macrocosm that affects the opportunities and resources available to children and their families and thus impacts child development through its prohibition or sanction of certain practices. In China, the most prominent institutions directly related to child well-being are the *hukou* system and the notorious family planning policies that have only recently been relaxed. These institutions have posed specific challenges to child development in China, as we describe below.

The hukou system and urban-rural divide

The *hukou* or household registration system categorizes a PRC national as either a "non-agricultural resident" (非农业户口) or an "agricultural resident" (农业户口). Though this system had ancient roots, it became solidified into a birth-ascribed system of social segmentation in the People's Republic of China during the Great Leap Forward.

As a set of policy tools for social and spatial control of the population, the *hukou* system ties people's access to public services and welfare such as education, employment, and health care to their "residential" status, leading to a *de facto* segregation between rural and urban residents (Chan and Zhang 1999; Wang 2005, 2010). Due to the urban bias in China's development policies, urban residents have been entitled to a range of social, economic, and cultural benefits that are mostly denied to rural residents, creating a significant urban-rural chasm and a large rural underclass. Until recently, the rigid *hukou* system greatly restricted the life chances of rural residents and erected major barriers to their residential and socio-economic mobility.

With the de-collectivization of the countryside in the early 1980s and the industrialization drive at full steam in most coastal cities, especially since the 1990s, laborers/workers from the countryside have not only worked in situ but have been allowed to seek jobs in private manufacturing companies, in retail and food services, and as construction workers for the booming urban infrastructure and housing sectors. However, the *hukou*-based governance system has severely limited rural migrant workers' civil rights and access to public services and welfare in their destination (urban) areas, such as housing, education, health care, and pensions (Solinger 1999; Whyte 2010). As members of the "floating population," most cannot obtain full urban resident status in the receiving cities, especially in large metropolitan areas such as Beijing and Shanghai. Therefore, their children are often denied access to urban public education system and have to attend underfunded low-quality private schools for migrant children, if these are available (Li 2015; Zhou and Cheung 2017). Even in urban areas where migrants outnumber local residents and contribute tremendously to local economic growth, the distribution of public resources is only intended for residents with local *hukou* status (Xiang 2007).

Partly in response to increasing public concern for the plight of migrant workers, the *hukou* system has been gradually reformed starting in the 1990s. "Temporary urban residence permits" for migrant workers to live and work legally in cities were adopted in most cities in the 1990s. Since 2001, various local governments have further adopted reform measures even though the reforms have not fundamentally changed the *hukou* system. The *hukou* system remains a formidable barrier to the integration of migrant workers in their destination cities and contributes to China's rural and urban disparity in access to social services (Chan and Buckingham 2008).

In 2014, the Legal Affairs Office of the State Council (China's cabinet) released a residence permit regulation intending to gradually replace the *hukou* system with a residence system that promises migrant workers equal treatment. One major goal of this reform is to ease the transition of more than 100 million migrant workers, who are mostly rural in *hukou* status, to urban resident status by the year 2020. However, while the new batch of policies encourage the development of smaller cities (with a population of fewer than one million) by opening their residence status to rural migrants, stringent conditions such as college education and stable employment are required for migrant workers to obtain urban residence status in large and mega cities.[1] As a large proportion of migrant workers and their families are concentrated in big cities and have low education levels and job insecurity, they will continue to have difficulty obtaining urban citizenship in the cities where they live and work.

Urbanization, migration, and the rural family structure

Despite the rural-urban divide created by the *hukou* system, migrant workers have contributed mightily to China's rapid industrialization and urbanization in the last three decades. According to the National Bureau of Statistics of China, the fraction of the population living in urban areas exceeded 50 percent in 2010 and by the end of 2015, about 56 percent of the total population lived in urban areas, up from 26 percent in 1990 (see Figure 2.1).

The massive migration of the rural labor force from countryside to cities has greatly contributed to this dramatic jump (Ren 2013).[2] However, due to the *hukou* barriers discussed above, few of the migrants can obtain permanent urban citizenship that entitles them to better-paying job opportunities and access to benefits such as affordable housing and children's education (Chan and Buckingham 2008). As of 2010, even though 50 percent of the total population in China lived in urban areas, only 29 percent of the population had urban *hukou* status. As a result, most migrant workers have to take poorly paid menial jobs shunned by urban residents, and their families have tended to live in crowded and often unsafe urban settings. According to the NBS, of the 168 million rural-urban migrant workers at the end of 2014, about

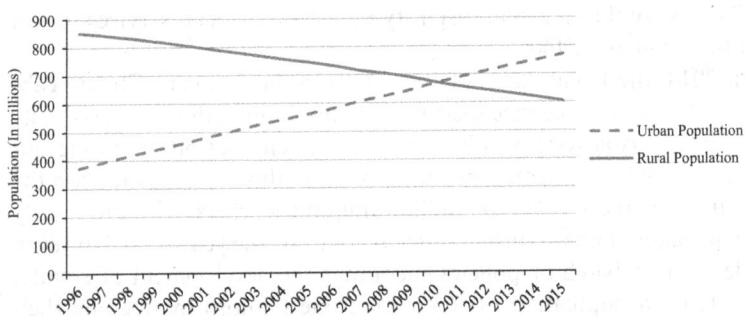

Figure 2.1 Rural vs. urban population in China, 1996–2015

Note: 1990, 2000, 2010 data are from the Census, based on permanent residence status. Data for the other years are estimates from annual population sample surveys, based on permanent residence status.

Source: National Bureau of Statistics of China.

130 million migrated alone and 35 million migrated with their families (NBS 2015). The children of the migrant workers are often left behind in the countryside, leading to the prevalence of split households in many rural areas (Guo and Huang 2014; Ma et al. 2011; Ye et al. 2013; Zhang and Zeng 2013).

Given this policy and institutional context, the children of migrant workers, whether they go with their parents to urban areas or are left behind in rural areas, have been significantly disadvantaged. According to NBS et al. (2017), by the end of 2015, there were around 34.3 million rural-to-urban migrant children (ages 0 and 17). They are faced with many institutional and cultural barriers to living in their destination cities, with the biggest challenge being limited access to education. In general, migrant children face formidable barriers to enrolling in local public schools (Pong 2014; Wu and Li 2017). With some exceptions, migrant children can only be admitted to local public schools if they pay extra fees and provide various documentation of their legal status, which most migrant families cannot afford. Although Chinese governments provides nine years of compulsory education (primary and middle schools), municipal governments offer free school education only to children with local *hukou* registrations, because they are reluctant to take on the extra cost for enrolling migrant children. Even if migrant children are fortunate enough to attend urban public schools in their destination cities, they have to return to their locales of origin where their *hukou* is registered to finish their high school education (Zhou and Cheung 2017). If they wish to enroll in college, they also need take the college entrance examination at their *hukou* residence (Ding 2012; Xiang 2007).

Aside from educational barriers, migrant children also suffer from other problems, including emotional difficulties such as low self-esteem and loneliness, behavioral problems such as smoking and drinking, and physical health problems such as a higher prevalence of infectious diseases (Hu et al. 2008; Luo 2005; Zhang, Qin, and Wu 2010). Needless to say, some of these physical and emotional issues are associated with the stresses related to poor educational access.

Children who are left behind in rural areas also encounter many challenges. According to NBS et al. (2017), there were more than 68.8 million left-behind children in China at the end of 2015, 25.4 percent of the total population of children. Unlike migrant children, the biggest challenge faced by left-behind children is the emotional distress due to absence of parents. As reported by the ACWF (2013), 46.74 percent of the left-behind children are left behind by both parents, of which 32.67 percent are living with their grandparents, 10.7 percent are living with others, typically relatives or friends of their parents, and 3.37 percent are living on their own.

While the money that migrant workers sent home has increased household income and enables the children left behind to cover school fees and obtain coveted material goods, parental migration also means that the children are bereft of parental support and supervision. Grandparents, often serving as primary guardians, usually have low literacy skills and limited energy to educate and take care of the left-behind children. As a result, left-behind children are susceptible to sub-par educational achievement and psychological difficulties as well as being at elevated risk of physical safety problems, human trafficking, and sexual harassment (Chen, Jiang, and Huang 2009; Pan and Ye 2014; Zheng and Wu 2014). However, there is also competing evidence indicating that parents' migration is not necessarily detrimental to child welfare and development, mainly due to return transfers of income and parents' recognition of the importance of education after migrating to urban cities (Fan et al. 2010; Ren and Treiman 2016; Wen and Lin 2012). Simply put, parental migration has been an important factor in child welfare and development of rural families for both left-behind and migrant children and is thus worthy of more comprehensive investigation.

Family planning policy and demographic transition

In addition to internal migration and urbanization, China's family planning policy has also had major influences on family structure and child development in China (Banister 2004; Fong 2006; Huang and Yang 2004). The Chinese government introduced this policy in 1979 to limit urban couples to only one child per couple and rural couples to have at most two births if the first child is a girl. With draconian enforcement of the family planning policy in most provinces, this policy, coupled with the effects of urbanization and modernization more generally, has contributed to the reduction of China's total fertility rate from 5.4 in 1971 to around 1.7 in the 1990s (Attané 2002; Wang et al. 2018).

The impact of the controversial family planning policy, also known as the "One-Child Policy," on child development has been intensely debated. According to Becker (1981), there is a negative correlation between the quantity of children and quality of their lives, indicating that lower fertility may encourage people to increase their investments in each child, including providing better education, more parenting time, and more emotional and financial support. In the case of China, academic findings generally support the positive effect of the quantity-quality tradeoff brought about by the one-child policy (Fong 2006;

Rosenzweig and Zhang 2009). It is good for child well-being in terms of greater parental investment and more available resources for children. Nonetheless, with the increasing prevalence of nuclear and stem families in China, the only children may be overwhelmed by the attention and expectation of their "helicopter" parents in urban areas (Quoss and Zhao 1995). Prior research has studied the psychological consequences experienced by children without siblings. Despite mixed conclusions, there is evidence that only children in China tend to be more self-centered, less independent, and less sociable than those with siblings. As a result, they have been called "little emperors" in China (Liu et al. 1988).

The impact of the one-child policy on China's sex ratio at birth (SRB) has been particularly noteworthy and has attracted much attention from demographers and society at large (Banister 2004). According to the NBS, China's SRB peaked in 2008 at a highly skewed 1.20, or 120 newborn boys for every 100 newborn girls, compared with the normal human sex ratio of 107 to 100. The SRB is higher in rural areas where societal preference for boys is stronger than in urban areas and fetal gender screening devices (ultrasound machines) were more easily accessible (Festini and de Martino 2004). Because of the selective abortion of female fetuses that is at least partly attributable to the imposition of the official birth planning policy, China today must cope with severe gender imbalances and a significant surplus of men. Nonetheless, with official restrictions on the number of children per couple, studies suggest that the (surviving) daughters have enjoyed unprecedented parental support and equal educational opportunities (Fong 2002; Tsui and Rich 2002).

As China's total fertility ratio has declined and life expectancy has increased, the shape of the Chinese population pyramid has changed dramatically since 1990 (Figure 2.2). Most striking is the dwindling number of school-age children over time, which is a major reason prompting local authorities to consolidate the number of schools in many areas, with inadvertent consequences for child well-being.

Education policy and child schooling

Following Mao's Cultural Revolution and the end of the Mao era, China began to rebuild its ravaged education system. In 1985, the Chinese government formulated a national policy for nine-year compulsory education for all school-aged children, though the implementation of this and other relevant policies were for many years enervated by extreme fiscal decentralization in educational financing (Wei and Yang 1997). It was not until the early 2000s that enrollment in primary schools became

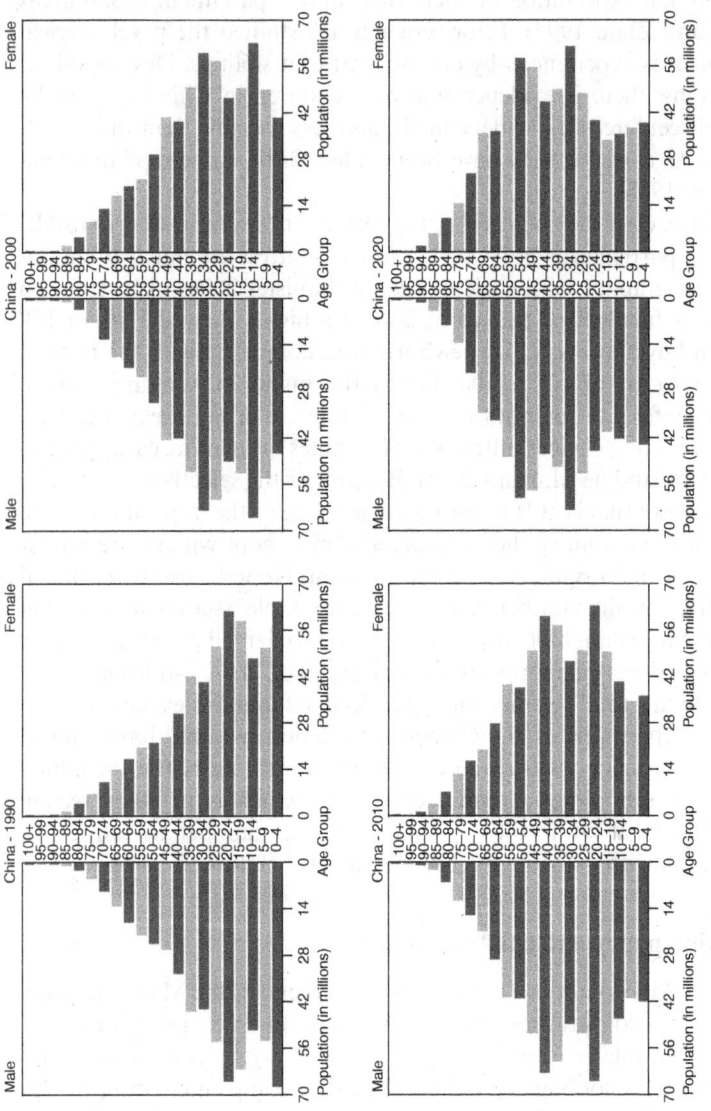

Figure 2.2 China's population pyramids 1990, 2000, 2010, 2020

Note: Sample-census population data by age and sex are used to evaluate the estimates and projections.

Source: International Data Base, United States Census Bureau (2017).

nearly universal and it would take another decade to do the same for middle school enrollment. As of 2002, for instance, the enrollment rates at the primary and middle school levels reached 98 percent and 90 percent respectively (Zhang and Zhao 2006). Implementation of the compulsory education policy has steadily boosted access to public education for rural children and helped narrow the urban-rural gap in basic schooling. However, considerable disparities still exist in government per-student spending, school resources and teaching quality between rural and urban areas (Tsang and Ding 2005).

Due to the changing demographic structure and emigration, a special challenge facing rural schools since the 2000s has been the decline in the number of school-aged children in rural areas. Partly in response to these trends and partly as a consequence of efforts to promote the mergers of villages and townships, the Chinese government launched a campaign for the "Adjustment of the Layout of Rural Schools," which called for rural school closures and consolidations (Lei 2010; Wan 2009). A major rationale for the campaign was to improve the efficient use of school resources through economies of scale by consolidating small rural schools into larger central schools and thus to improve teaching quality and equity (Fang and Liu 2013; Xu 2013). A majority of village primary schools, external teaching sites, and one-room type village school houses were closed and the pupils were transferred into "central" schools located in townships and county seats.

As a result of the school consolidation movement, the number of schools in rural areas has decreased steadily (Fig. 2.3). In 2000, there were 440,000 rural primary schools in China. Ten years later, this number

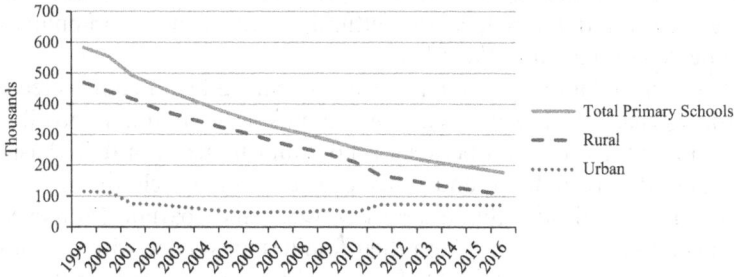

Figure 2.3 Number of primary schools in China, 1999–2016

Notes: Primary schools exclude adult primary schools and external teaching sites. Urban primary schools include those in both urban areas and counties/towns.

Source: Ministry of Education of China.

had decreased to 230,000—a decrease of over 50 percent (21st Century Education Institute 2013). Between 2000 and 2010, an average of 63 primary schools, 30 teaching sites and 3 middle schools disappeared each day in rural areas. The number of external teaching sites hit its lowest point in 2010.

The school consolidation campaign was called off in 2012 because of public criticism of its controversial effects on child education (Liu et al. 2009). In 2012, the State Council issued a document titled "Statements on Promoting the Balanced Development of Compulsory Education" to promote rural education quality through more government investment in school facilities, teacher training and technological innovation (State Council 2012). In recent years, the number of external teaching sites has risen steadily as the much larger central schools have developed such sites to better serve pupils spatially.

On the positive side, the school consolidation policy appears to have been partially effective. It may have boosted educational efficiency through economies of scale (Fan and Guo 2009; Li, Zeng, and Yang 2012) and improved education quality and promoted regional equity (Fang and Liu 2013; Ma, Lu, and Li 2011).

Critics of the school consolidation policy, however, have pointed to a variety of adverse effects the policy has had on rural children's development. Most obviously, the school consolidation has dramatically increased the distance students in remote areas needed to travel to get to school, leading to higher transportation costs and higher vehicle safety risks (Chu and Zhang 2012; Ke, Xu, and Zhang 2015; Yi et al. 2012). As a result, there was an increase in the drop-out rates for some segments of the rural student population living in remote areas. The closure of village schools also removes these schools as local anchor institutions in these villages and thus reduces the cultural vitality of these communities (Xiong 2009; Zhao and Wu 2015).

The consolidation of schools was accompanied by a major increase in the number of students living on campus as it became impossible for many pupils to travel between school and home on a daily basis. However, due to funding and other problems, many schools in rural areas have dormitories that are over-crowded and spartan. Moreover, young children living away from their families must cope with psychological stresses due to the lack of parental supervision and emotional support (Cui 2012). Taken together, the dramatic increase in the use of school dormitories has effectively turned many schools into boarding schools and has had detrimental effects on students' physical and psychological health (Chu and Zhang 2012; Wan 2009).

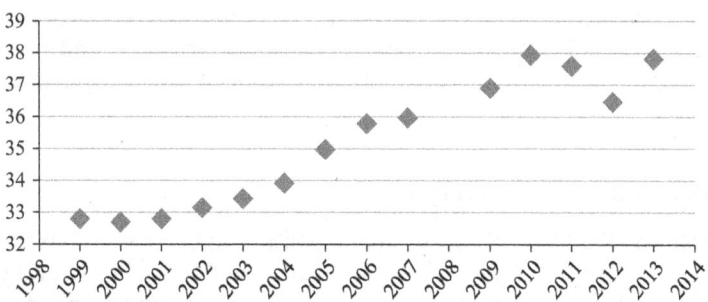

Figure 2.4 Primary school class size in China, 1999–2013
Source: Ministry of Education of China.

In addition, school consolidation has also led to larger classes in the central schools. According to data from the Ministry of Education of China, the average primary school class size increased from about 33 in 2000 to 37–38 in the 2010s (Figure 2.4). Such large classes make it harder for teachers to manage their classes and can be detrimental to teaching quality (Fang and Liu 2013; Tao and Lu, 2011).

Hence, despite the promise of promoting educational equity, the effect of the policy has been to further exacerbate the disparities between remote villages in the county periphery and urban areas in the county core (Cai and Kong 2014; Fan and Hao 2011; Xu 2013). To address these problems, the Chinese government launched a "no tuition and no fee" national policy and has also required central schools to provide school shuttle services, with mixed results (Xu 2013). The establishment of more external teaching sites in recent years is thus another effort to address the adverse effects of school consolidation.

The urban-rural differences in access to education are also apparent for early childhood education. While government-sponsored and private kindergartens have been widely available for urban residents, early childhood education was largely neglected in most rural areas due to lack of funding and qualified teachers. It was not until 2010 that the Chinese government began to address the issue by encouraging the opening of more kindergartens, public or private. In its "National Guideline on the Mid- and Long-term Plan for Educational Reform and Development," the Chinese government set the ambitious goal that, by 2020, the kindergarten enrollment rate for preschool children should reach 70 percent, 80 percent and 95 percent respectively for children three years, two years and one year prior to school age. As a result, rural kindergartens have mushroomed in the last decade (Qi and Melhuish 2017). Not surprisingly, the rapid growth in the number of kindergartens in rural areas has been complicated by concerns with undertrained teachers and poor facilities (Hu et al. 2016).

Health care system and reform

China during the Mao era saw dramatic political upheavals such as the Great Leap Forward and the Cultural Revolution that also profoundly impacted health and longevity of the population. By the end of the Mao era, however, China had developed a basic public health care system with a network of local state-owned health care facilities and public health care workforce. In most rural communities, local health workers called "bare-foot doctors" were employed to provide basic health care services at the village level. The basic health care system together with investment in public health, increasing availability of new medicine and procedures contributed to improvement in the health conditions of the population, including children.

With market-oriented economic reforms since the 1980s, government funding of the health care sector in rural areas has been curtailed. While many urban Chinese could rely on the government or employer-based insurance programs to cover most of the medical care cost, rural residents until recently had to bear the cost themselves without any insurance coverage (Blumenthal and Hsiao 2015). In the first decade of this century, facing vociferous public complaints about increasing medical cost, the Chinese government introduced the new rural cooperative medical insurance scheme with the support of government subsidies on insurance premium payment (Meng, Tao, and Liu 2004). As of 2014, 95 percent of the rural population were covered under the scheme. Despite its limitations, including co-pay requirements, the rural medical insurance system has helped prevent some rural families from slipping into poverty due to high medical expenses. The government has also worked to set up a health care delivery system in rural areas with township hospitals and village clinics.

Although rising incomes together with government efforts have increased the health status of rural population, rural urban disparity in health care services and health status still persists (Yin 2008). Whereas China has enjoyed significant improvements in most of its health indicators, including infant mortality and life expectancy, recent data indicates that in 2013, the under-five death rate, infant mortality and newborn death rate in rural areas are 1.4, 1.2 and 1 times higher than in urban areas (UNICEF 2014).

Conclusion

Against the background of rapid economic growth that has significantly improved Chinese living standards and elevated China's economic status globally, we need to keep in mind a number of major policy and institutional parameters as we examine child development and well-being in contemporary China. These include the continuing relevance of the *hukou* or household registration system, the massive number of migrant workers, especially from rural to urban settings, the imposition and consequences of strict birth planning policies, and changes in education and health policies.

Notes

1 In recent years, various forms of migration point system were adopted in many big cities that emphasize high education, stable employment, and homeownership. These requirements have effectively banned most migrant workers from the opportunity of becoming an urban resident.
2 Besides the influx of migrants, the en masse reclassification of many rural areas surrounding central cities and many rural towns as urban has also raised the percentage of urban population (see Ren 2013 for details).

3 Economic well-being

Economic well-being is a multi-dimensional concept and refers to the material resources and conditions available to children in their immediate living environment (such as in their families). While various aspects of economic well-being in family and social contexts are not domains of child development, they have a major and direct impact on child development. Generally speaking, whereas we celebrate those who rise from rags to riches, all too often material scarcity profoundly shapes the lives of youths (Mullainathan and Shafir 2014). Persistent family economic hardship and early material deprivation may cause malnutrition and thus affect children's physical health such as stunted growth. They can also result in toxic influences on family processes and parenting and produce long-term detrimental effects on children's socioemotional and cognitive development (Bradley and Corwyn 2002; Hamoudi, Murray, Sorensen, and Fountaine 2014; Linver, Brooks-Gunn, and Kohen 2002; Yeung, Linver, and Brooks-Gunn 2002).

Eradicating extreme poverty is one of the United Nation's eight Millennium Development Goals (MDGs).[1] Despite China's rapid economic development for the past four decades, at the end of 2012 there were still nearly 100 million people living below the poverty line of 2,300 Yuan per capita annual net income.[2] The poorest people are concentrated in rural communities that often lack basic hygiene, infrastructure, and health care facilities. Regional disparities in poverty rate of the rural population are striking, at 12.4 percent, 7.5 percent and 2.7 percent respectively for the western, central and eastern provinces (NBS 2015). Of all age groups, children under 15 years old have the highest poverty rate.

In this short chapter, we draw on the CFPS data to examine the economic well-being, including the living conditions, of Chinese children, with special attention to those living in poverty. We selected nine indicators of economic conditions. Besides family poverty based on per capita net income and house crowding, we also include access to tap drinking water, clean cooking fuel, flush toilet, and trash collection facilities. These factors have a major impact on population health and have been used by the UN and Chinese government as major indicators of deprivation (Qi and Wu 2014; UNICEF 2014). Parents' high school education is used to suggest parents' employment prospects and earning power in the labor market. Receipt of government aid indicates the availability of government financial assistance for those in need. We pay special attention to rural-urban disparities in various dimensions of economic well-being. We also examine the family economic status of children in different living arrangements, including rural children who are left behind by one or both migrant parents, and migrant children living with their parents in urban areas.

Economic well-being and rural-urban disparities

As shown in Table 3.1, 22 percent of Chinese children live below the poverty line of 2,300 Yuan per capita as of 2014. More than one-third of the children live in households with no access to tap water, clean fuel for cooking, flush toilet, or trash collection service. Parental education levels in China are still fairly low. 75 percent of fathers and 78 percent of mothers did not graduate from high school.

Table 3.1 Children's family economic conditions by community type, 2014

Variables	Community type		
	Rural (%)	Urban (%)	Total (%)
Family in poverty*	21.9	8.5	18.2
House crowding	17.8	16.9	17.5
No tap water for cooking*	42.8	5.9	32.5
No clean fuel for cooking*	46.6	8.5	36.0
No flush toilet*	65.9	19.1	52.8
No trash collection service*	52.6	6.6	39.8
Father's education less than high school*	84.1	51.8	74.9
Mother's education less than high school*	87.8	54.9	78.5
Receiving government aid	14.9	7.1	12.7

Note: CFPS child sample $N = 8,312$, results are weighted. * $p < .05$ based on design-based Pearson chi-square statistic. * indicates statistically significant difference between rural and urban children. House crowding is indicated for at least one of the following situations: children above 12 years old share the same bedroom with their parents, three generations share the same bedroom, children of the opposite sex above 12 years old share the same bedroom, beds set up in the living room, or beds only set up at night.

Table 3.2 Changes in children's family economic conditions, 2010 to 2014

Difference	Rural (%)	Urban (%)	Total (%)
Family in poverty	−3.8	−0.8	−3.1
House crowding	−2.4	0.0	−1.8
No tap water for cooking	−16.1*	−3.5	−13.1
No clean fuel for cooking	−18.0*	−6.6*	−15.3
Not use flush toilet	−10.8*	−4.3	−9.6
No trash collection service	−25.0*	−3.7	−19.8
Father's education less than high school	−4.2*	−3.5	−4.5
Mother's education less than high school	−5.5*	−6.4*	−6.3
Receiving government aid	4.9†	0.5	3.6

Note: CFPS child sample $N = 8{,}312$ in 2014, and $N = 8{,}990$ in 2010.
* $p < .05$, † $p < 0.1$ based on design-based Pearson chi-square. * indicates significant change between 2010 and 2014 for rural or urban children. Results are weighted.

Table 3.2 compares changes in the above indicators between 2010, the year of the CFPS baseline survey, and 2014. In national policy terms, this relatively brief period stands out for the substantial changes in most of the indicators. Compared to the 2010 results, the number of children in households with access to tap water, clean fuel for cooking, flush toilet, and a trash collection service has greatly increased. It is also worth noting that the percentage of children in poverty and house crowding has decreased. The economic well-being for both rural and urban children saw substantial improvement between 2010 and 2014, and the improvement for the rural families concerning tap water, clean fuel, and sanitation was especially prominent.

Table 3.2 shows that, due to rapid economic improvement in rural living conditions, the urban-rural gap has narrowed considerably between 2010 and 2014. However, as shown in Figure 3.1, with the exception of housing crowding, the rural-urban disparity in the other indicators is apparent and stark. A much higher percentage of rural children do not have access to tap water and sanitation facilities at home. 84 percent of rural fathers and 88 percent of rural mothers have less than high school education versus 52 percent and 55 percent respectively for urban parents.

Economic well-being of children in different living arrangements

Table 3.3 presents detailed breakdowns of data by the children's family living arrangements. As is to be expected, children in urban intact

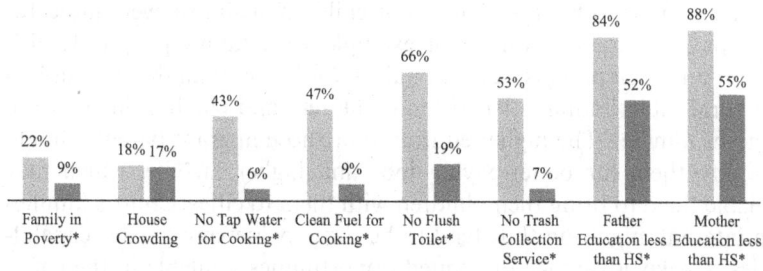

Figure 3.1 Children's family economic conditions, 2014
Note: * p < .05 based on design-based Pearson chi-square statistic.
Source: CFPS (2014).

Table 3.3 Children's family economic conditions by living arrangement, 2014

Variables	Rural intact (%)	Urban intact (%)	LBC-no parent (%)	LBC-1 parent (%)	Migrant (%)	Single-parent/orphan (%)
Family in poverty*	22.6	8.6	19.3	17.4	14.0	18.4
House crowding*	18.2	14.4	16.4	15.7	18.7	25.1
No tap water*	39.8	6.0	46.5	40.8	26.2	30.8
No clean fuel*	42.4	8.6	54.0	44.0	26.0	43.3
No flush toilet*	63.7	20.7	61.5	62.4	36.9	57.8
No trash collection service*	47.8	5.9	59.8	52.2	31.9	42.0
Father's education less than high school*	84.4	50.1	76.0	82.1	65.4	79.2
Mother's education less than high school*	87.7	53.5	85.8	85.1	66.8	78.6
Receiving government aid	12.9	6.7	13.7	16.3	7.8	28.6

Note: CFPS child sample N = 8,312, results are weighted. * p < .05 based on design-based Pearson chi-square statistic.
* indicates significant differences in the indicators between two or more of the six living arrangements.

families have better family financial and living conditions as well as higher parental education levels. Interestingly, although less well-off than children in urban intact families, migrant children are still doing better than the other three groups of children in almost every indicator except for house crowding. For example, their family poverty level is lower and their parents' educational level is higher than that of children in rural intact families, left-behind children, and children in single/no parent families. The higher education of those migrant parents should qualify them for better-paying jobs and higher income, which may enable them to bring their children with them to cities. China's families in internal migration thus tend to be those possessing greater capabilities to take advantage of limited opportunities available in their new locales.

In view of the many media reports about the difficulties facing left-behind children, it is notable that, in terms of economic well-being, left-behind children with either one or both migrant parents in rural areas are somewhat better off on the family poverty indicator than those in families with both parents around. Obviously, remittances by migrant parents have helped improve the economic status of the rural left-behind children. This is in line with findings of prior studies of rural families in various regions of China (Zhou, Murphy, and Tao 2014). However, compared to rural intact families, left-behind children with both migrant parents suffer more from a lack of access to tap water, clean fuel, and trash collection services. This is partly due to the higher concentration of children with both parents absent in poor rural communities of central and western regions. Compared to eastern regions, these communities often lack resources to improve drinking water and trash collection services for the local residents.

Unlike in 2010, when the children from single/no parent families are found to be the most economically disadvantaged, in 2014 the poverty rate for children with single/no parent is similar to children left behind and in rural intact families, although they are more likely to live in crowded housing conditions (see Table 3.3). It is also worth noting that children in single/no parent families are better off than those left-behind and in rural intact families in terms of access to tap water, clean fuel for cooking, flush toilet and trash collection services. These results reflect the fact that the children from single/no parent families include both rural and urban residents while the left-behind children are overwhelmingly rural and located in less-developed central and western regions of China.

Table 3.4 shows that between 2010 and 2014, the economic well-being of children of all living arrangements improved substantially.

Table 3.4 Changes in children's family economic conditions by living arrangement, 2010 to 2014

Variables	Rural intact (%)	Urban intact (%)	LBC-no parent (%)	LBC-1 parent (%)	Migrant (%)	Single/No parent (%)
Family in poverty*	−2.0	1.5	−9.7	−4.8	1.6	−15.6
House crowding	−2.7	−1.3	0.8	−1.8	−1.5	−2.1
No tap water for cooking*	−15.9	−2.7	−13.4	−18.7	−2.1	−9.7
No clean fuel for cooking*	−18.4	−6.3	−16.0	−18.5	−1.7	−14.4
No flush toilet*	−12.1	−2.9	−12.0	−10.1	1.9	−2.9
No trash collection service*	−26.1	−2.6	−19.9	−23.8	−0.9	−16.7
Father's education less than high school*	−4.1	−1.2	−9.8	−0.2	−5.5	−3.8
Mother's education less than high school*	−5.8	−4.8	−5.5	−3.2	−8.3	−5.7
Receiving government aid*	3.6	0.6	3.2	8.5	2.2	5.3

Note: Numbers are 2014 percentage minus 2010 percentage. CFPS child sample $N = 8,312$ in 2014, $N = 8,990$ in 2010. Results are weighted. * $p < .05$, † $p < 0.1$ based on design-based Pearson chi-square. * indicates significant change between 2010 and 2014 for one or more of the six living arrangements.

It is remarkable that the living conditions for rural children, including children in rural intact and left-behind families, and children in single/no parent families improved by more than 10 percentage points. Now the majority of families have access to tap water, clean fuel for cooking and trash collection service. In addition, a higher percentage of families are receiving government aid, reflecting the reach of the Chinese government's targeted poverty alleviation programs.

Conclusion

As a result of China's extraordinary economic expansion and vigorous efforts by the Chinese leadership to promote more inclusive development, more and more of the Chinese population have enjoyed the fruits of China's economic progress. The rising tide of development has lifted all boats. While China has also joined the ranks of highly unequal societies, official statistics show that the income gap between rich and poor in China peaked at the end of 2000s and has declined after 2010 (Han, Zhao, and Zhao 2016; Xie and Zhou 2014).

Measured in the economic well-being of children, our data reveal rapid improvement for families in all categories after 2010. Improvement of children's living conditions has also benefited from the various development programs implemented by the central and local governments to boost rural sanitation and health conditions. Several studies have examined the implementation and positive effect of government programs such as supply of safe drinking water and installation of sanitary toilets in rural China (Cheng et al. 2018; Meng, Tao, and Liu 2004). That said, rural-urban disparities in children's economic conditions are still striking enough to merit our continuous attention.

Notes

1 See the MDG's website at: www.un.org/millenniumgoals/ for details.
2 The rural poverty line of 2,300 Yuan per year is equivalent to 1.6 USD per person per day based on Purchasing Power Parity exchange rate in 2005 and 1.8 USD at the 2015 PPP exchange rate. See NBS (2015). According to the *Poverty Monitoring Report of Rural China* (NBS 2015), the Chinese poverty line for rural areas is set above the World Bank's world poverty line of 1.25 USD for absolute poverty (meeting basic needs for food and clothing necessary for long-term physical health). It is similar to the World Bank's relative poverty line of 2.00 USD per day (adequate for a stable life of sufficient food and clothing as well as adequate shelter in rural areas).

4 Physical well-being

As the most visible aspect of child well-being, physical well-being is itself comprised of multiple dimensions, among which are physical activity, incidence of disease and hospitalization, age- and gender-appropriate body mass index (BMI), and healthy lifestyle (Moore et al. 2008). Physical health is the foundation of children's overall development and affects all other domains of child well-being. Physical health indicators such as birthweight, infant mortality rate, and nutrition status are included in health promotion policies and intervention programs in China (for instance, see "Chinese Children Development Program 2011–2020" released by the State Council, 2011b). As indicated by official statistics, the physical health status of Chinese children has greatly improved in the past half century with the increasing availability of health care services and better living conditions (Meng, Tao, and Liu 2014; UNICEF 2014). This short chapter draws on data from the 2010 and 2014 CFPS surveys to describe aspects of children's physical health in China. We cover the following indicators: the rate of low birthweight children, incidence of sickness and hospitalization, health insurance coverage, overweight and underweight, self-reported health and regular exercise behavior.

Child health in rural and urban areas

The World Health Organization defines low birthweight as weighing less than 2.5 kilograms (5.5 pounds) at birth for the infants (UNICEF and WHO 2004).[1] As birthweight in the CFPS survey is reported by the caregiver instead of actual measurements, we restrict the sample to zero to three year olds in order to minimize recall bias. The incidence of sickness in the past month and hospitalization in the past year for a child are also based on caregiver reports and thus subject to recall bias. For health status and lifestyle for children who are 10 to 15 years old, we

Table 4.1 Children's health conditions by community type, 2014

Variables	Community type		Total (%)
	Rural (%)	Urban (%)	
Low birthweight (0–3 years old)	4.3	2.3	3.7
Sick last month (0–3 years old)	44.5	44.5	44.5
Saw doctor last year (0–15 years old)	49.8	51.5	50.3
Hospitalized last year (0–15 years old)	8.3	9.8	8.8
Have medical insurance (0–15 years old)	67.5	64.8	66.7
Self-reported health (10–15 years old)*	91.4	94.5	92.4
Exercised last month (10–15 years old)*	71.4	78.8	73.7
BMI categories (3–15 years old)*			
Underweight	18.5	16.5	17.9
Normal	49.7	57.7	52.1
Overweight	9.4	11.1	9.9
Obese	22.4	14.8	20.1

Note: Sample size varies according to age groups. Results are weighted percentages.
* $p < .05$ based on design-based Pearson chi-square statistic.

use as indicators self-reported health status and frequency of physical exercise in the past month.

Table 4.1 shows that low birthweight children accounted for 3.7 percent of all zero to three-year-olds in 2014. The low birthweight rates for rural and urban areas were 4.3 and 2.3 respectively, although the difference does not reach statistically significant levels. Our results are similar to the low birthweight rates reported in a study based on the 2013 National Health Services Survey in China (NHFPC 2015).[2] Poverty, malnutrition, lack of prenatal care, and poor living and working conditions may have contributed to low birthweight (Kramer 1987; Tang et al. 2017). For comparison, according to the US Centers for Disease Control and Prevention, the percentage of children born with low birthweight in the US was 8.17 percent in 2016 (based on hospital birth records). Allowing for differences in measurement, it is nonetheless interesting to know that the Chinese low birthweight indicator based on the CFPS compares well with the US figure, which tends to be an outlier among developed countries.

The CFPS 2014 data reveals that, according to their caregivers, 44.5 percent of the children aged zero to three had fallen sick "in the last month." The sickness incidence rate was similar for urban and rural children. Our estimate is much higher than the two-week disease incidence rate for children (9.6 and 12.5 percent respectively for infants and one year old in past two weeks) reported by NHFPC (2013). This may be due to NHFPC's more strict definition of "being sick."[3] The percentage of all children (0 to 15 years old) having seen a doctor due to illness or being hospitalized in the past year is also similar between rural and urban areas in 2014.

While there are some urban-rural differences in reported health status for older children (10 to 15 years old), the differences are modest. Rural children are less likely to engage in physical exercise twice or more in the last month (71 percent vs. 79 percent).

Based on the CFPS 2014 data, 68 percent of the children in urban areas and 65 percent in rural areas were covered by medical insurance programs.[4] Most of the medical insurance programs are publicly funded. The increase in insurance coverage is most striking for children in urban areas with an increase of 8 percentage points from 2010 to 2014.[5]

Another major indicator of child physical soundness is the body mass index (BMI), which is a person's weight in kilograms divided by the square of height in meters. Since a high BMI often indicates high body fat, BMI can be used to screen for weight categories such as obese or overweight that may be associated with health issues. Because China's national BMI standards for children by age and gender only apply to children seven years and older (WGOC 2004), we used the US CDC's (Center for Disease Control and Prevention) child growth standards instead, though we also referred to the WHO child growth standards.[6] We calculated each child's BMI percentile from its gender- and age-specific BMI and classified the children into four categories: obese (≥ 95th percentile), overweight (85th to 95th percentile), normal (5th to 85th percentile) and underweight (≤ 5th percentile).

As shown in Table 4.1, in 2014, 18.5 percent of rural children and 16.5 percent of urban children aged three to fifteen years old are underweight. Remarkably, 22 percent of the rural children are in the obese category, compared to 15 percent of the urban children. As a result, only 50 percent of the rural children have a BMI within the normal weight range, compared to 58 percent of the urban children.

The early 2010s were years of exuberance in China when much of the rest of the world was mired in recession. Even though only four years elapsed between 2010 and 2014, the changes in the health conditions of Chinese children during that period are illuminating: the total low birthweight rate decreased; and the rural-urban disparity in the low birthweight rate, although still observed in 2014, narrowed (Table 4.2).

Another encouraging finding is that, in both urban and rural areas, the percentage of children with health insurance coverage saw a dramatic increase so that the rate of insurance coverage for both groups became

Table 4.2 Changes in children's health conditions, 2010 to 2014

Variables	Community type		
	Rural (%)	Urban (%)	Total (%)
Low birthweight (0–3 years old)	–1.5	–0.5	–1.3
Sick last month (0–3 years old)	–2.8	+1.3	–1.7
Saw doctor last year	–0.4	–4.7	–1.6
Hospitalized last year	+0.7	+1.1	+0.8
Have medical insurance	+7.3*	+13.8*	+9.0
BMI categories (3–15 years old)			
Underweight	–1.9	–3.0	–2.3
Normal	+0.3	–0.2	+0.2
Overweight	+0.6	+1.1	+0.7
Obese	+1.1	+2.1	+1.3

Note: Sample sizes vary according to age group, results are weighted. * $p < .05$ based on design-based Pearson chi-square statistic, indicating significant change from 2010 to 2014.

similar (67.5 percent vs. 64.8 percent). This reflected the rapid increase in the rate of enrollment in the New Rural Cooperative Medical Scheme (NRCMS) and the health insurance schemes for urban residents after 2003, when NRCMS was introduced (NHFPC 2015). Despite the progress made, we should take note that a third of the rural and urban children still had no medical insurance coverage as of 2014. Nonetheless, these insurance schemes have continued to expand in recent years and the rate of coverage is expected to have further increased.

Another positive sign, as shown in Table 4.2, is that the proportion of underweight children has decreased in both rural and urban areas. However, the proportion of children with obesity has also increased. This is in line with the general trend of declining underweight rates and increasing obesity in the last three decades, as reported by Zong and Li (2014).

Just as low-income groups in the US have had greater difficulty with nutrition and health and have had more (over-)weight issues, it is not contradictory that the rate of obesity is higher for children in rural than urban areas as the rural population has only recently left behind subsistence conditions and has rapidly gained access to a surfeit of calories. Zhang et al. (2016) attributed the rapid increase in child obesity and overweight in rural areas to their different eating habits, food preferences and lack of physical exercise. Zong and Li (2014) also observe that rates of overweight/obesity and stunting are both at high levels in China's poorer western provinces. This is believed to be a result of protein and energy malnutrition that increases body weight without corresponding improvements in height, thus causing the BMI to increase.

Physical health of children in different living arrangements

Family structure and living arrangements are important for children. As the data in Table 4.3 show, a key finding is that infants and toddlers younger than three years old are much more vulnerable to illnesses if both parents leave them behind or if they migrate with their parents even though they fare well on the low birthweight indicator. The deficit of parental care for the infants and toddlers at home, including the absence of breast-feeding, would have contributed to the higher levels of morbidity for this group. If these infants and toddlers migrate with their parents, they would have to cope with poor living conditions and still inadequate parent supervision and thus more likely to suffer from the viruses they are exposed to.

The left-behind children aged 10 to 15 years old with no parent present are also least likely to have exercised in the last month, followed by children with only one parent at home. Children with no parent at home are the most likely to be obese or underweight.

Table 4.3 Children's health conditions by living arrangement, 2014

Variables	Rural intact (%)	Urban intact (%)	LBC-no parent (%)	LBC-1 parent (%)	Migrant (%)	Single-parent/orphan (%)
Low birthweight (0–3) †	4.6	2.3	0.6	5.9	0.7	4.6
Sick last month (0–3) †	43.2	40.5	53.8	44.9	57.5	34.0
Saw doctor last year	49.1	51.0	51.7	53.4	55.5	50.7
Hospitalized last year	8.1	9.8	9.2	12.1	7.0	6.9
Have medical insurance	67.2	66.5	72.2	67.0	59.6	61.0
Self-reported healthy (10–15)	92.1	95.0	92.8	89.7	93.4	89.3
Exercise last month (10–15)*	72.0	81.4	65.4	67.0	72.3	77.7
BMI categories (3–15)*						
Underweight	18.7	16.4	19.1	17.6	18.9	14.8
Normal	50.7	58.8	44.9	53.5	48.8	52.2
Overweight	9.1	10.1	11.4	8.9	13.2	10.9
Obese	21.6	14.7	24.6	20.0	19.1	22.1

Note: Sample sizes vary based on age group. Results weighted.
† $.05 < p < .10$; * $p < .05$ based on design-based Pearson chi-square statistic.

Table 4.4 Changes in children's health conditions by living arrangement, 2010 to 2014

Variables	Rural intact (%)	Urban intact (%)	LBC- no parent (%)	LBC-1 parent (%)	Migrant (%)	Single-parent/ orphan (%)
Low birthweight (0–3)†	–1.0	+0.4	–5.7	–0.3	–3.1	–3.1
Sick last month (0–3)†	–0.4	+1.5	–8.0	–8.3	+14.3	–26.2
Saw doctor last year†	+1.1	–5.5	–9.4	–1.9	+4.9	+2.1
Hospitalized last year	+0.9	+1.6	+0.4	+2.2	–1.8	–0.5
Have Medical Insurance*	+5.7	+13.9	+14.1	+8.6	+18.0	+1.5
BMI categories (2–15)*						
Underweight	–1.8	–2.1	+1.3	–5.5	–1.7	–7.2
Normal	+1.1	+0.7	–1.9	+0.7	–8.3	+1.1
Overweight	–0.3	–0.2	+3.3	+2.0	+4.7	+0.4
Obese	+1.0	+1.5	–2.7	+2.8	+5.3	+5.7

Note: Numbers are 2014 percentage minus 2010 percentage.
* $p < .05$, † $p < 0.1$ based on design-based Pearson chi-square.
* indicates significant change between 2010 and 2014 for one or more of the six living arrangements.

Table 4.4 allows us to compare changes between 2014 and 2010. What stands out in the data is the increase in access to public health insurance across the board for all six groups of children. Migrant children have benefited the most with a large 16 percentage point increase in public medical insurance coverage, although it still has the least proportion of children insured.

Compared to 2010, left-behind children with either no parent or one parent at home are much less likely to be sick in 2014. Meanwhile, migrant children have seen an increased chance of getting sick (43.3 percent vs. 57.5 percent), making this group the most susceptible to illnesses. Migrant children, and children orphaned or with a single parent have seen a large increase in the proportion of being overweight or obese.

Summary and discussion

In the early 2010s, the physical health conditions of Chinese children improved appreciably in terms of birthweight and morbidity for rural children. In addition to the better living conditions for rural children, access to public health insurance also significantly improved for all children, especially for left-behind children and migrant children. In 2014, over 70 percent of left-behind children with no parents at home had access to medical insurance, the highest among all the other groups. However, only less than 60 percent of migrant children have access to medical insurance. Low participation of migrant children in medical insurance partly reflects the lack of portability of NRCMS across regions and the policy barriers erected by host cities against health service provision to migrant children (Wang et al. 2014; Zhuo et al. 2007). With rising incomes and better access to health insurance, positive improvements in health outcomes are observed and some of the improvements are quite striking for such a relatively short time period.

Despite progress being made, there are also setbacks. While the low birthweight indicator has improved for all groups of children, obesity has become a growing problem, especially for rural children. The rate of obesity for children in rural intact families and left-behind has surpassed that of urban intact children. It is most prevalent among the rural left-behind children with no parent present, with a quarter of them being obese. One risk factor may be the lack of physical exercise for the left-behind children, as our analysis indicates. Prior studies of child obesity in China have also confirmed that left behind children who are often taken care of by their grandparents have a much higher probability to be obese (Li et al. 2015). Due to their low education, grandparents often have inappropriate perceptions and knowledge about child obesity (e.g., fat children are healthy) and mistaken ideas about food contents (high fat content is more nutritious) and eating behavior (overfeeding and lack of exercise). Further interventions are required to target grandparent and other child caregivers and raise their awareness about the hazards of child obesity.

Notes

1 China's National Health and Family Planning Commission (NHFPC) sets the low birthweight standard differently for boys (2.5 kilograms) and girls (2.4 kilograms) (NHFPC 2015).
2 The NHFPC reported low birthweight rates for rural and urban newborns are respectively 3.4 and 3.3 in 2013 (NHFPC, 2013). Our low birthweight rate estimate for urban areas is lower probably because we use a narrower definition of "urban" based on administrative categorization of communities. Several recent studies based on birth records collected from hospitals and health facilities in China estimate the low birthweight rate of infants as 6.1 percent in 2011 (Chen et al. 2013) and 5.36 percent on average between 2012 and 2014 (Tang et al. 2017). Their much higher estimates than our results may arise from a variety of reasons, including (1) their overrepresentation of large hospitals and health facilities enables them to capture relatively more

difficult (e.g., Cesarean-section) and premature births that tend to occur in large hospitals instead of rural health clinics, (2) the possible recall bias of caregivers in the CFPS sample.
3 According the NHFPC definition, the reported sickness needs to meet one of the three conditions: (1) having seen a doctor, (2) needing medical treatment or auxiliary treatment, and (3) needing rest from work and school and stay in bed for at least a day (infants and toddlers abnormal crying and fussing and loss of appetite, etc.).
4 Public health insurance programs include New Rural Cooperative Medical Scheme (NRCMS), urban employee health insurance, and urban resident health insurance. Only 10 percent of the children were also covered by private or commercial medical insurance plans (Chen, Jiang, & Huang 2009).
5 Official statistics in China indicate that the new rural cooperative medical care system has covered over 90 percent of the rural population by 2008 and further reached 96 percent of the rural population in 2011 (832 million). The 2013 NHFPC report based on the National Health Services Survey also shows a very high percentage of people with medical insurance (97.3 and 92.8 percent respectively for rural and urban residents). One study has called into question the reliability of official estimates (Yu 2009) because local government may forge enrollment numbers of NRCMS in order to receive central government subsidies for premium payments. Another reason for the large difference between our estimates and official statistics may be because families are unable or unwilling to enroll their children in health insurance programs for various reasons (Zhuo et al. 2007).
6 We also tried to use the WHO child growth standards to calculate the weight classifications of the children and the results are similar.

5 Psychological and social well-being

Psychological well-being and social well-being are two separate, but related, developmental domains for children. Psychological health refers to the mental and emotional state of children and their opinions about themselves and their future. Indicators include self-esteem, self-efficacy, psychological distress, sense of happiness and confidence about the future. Social well-being indicates the ability and skills of children to get along with others and make friends in their social milieu. The two domains are closely related because children with mental problems—such as depression, anxiety, and other emotional self-regulation disturbances—often act out in socially undesirable ways, such as showing social withdrawal, aggressiveness, or antisocial behaviors. Children and adolescents with mental health issues and social deficits often have difficulty in normal cognitive development and school performance (see, for example, Breslau et al. 2008).

The US CDC has been monitoring children's mental health in the US through various ongoing national surveys and registry systems (Centers for Disease Control and Prevention, 2013). Although there are no comprehensive national statistics about children's mental and social health state in China, existing studies have examined various mental health issues of vulnerable children and youth in different regions of China (e.g., Knight, Song, and Gunatilaka 2009; Ren and Treiman 2016; Tang and Qin 2015; Wen, Su, Li, and Lin 2015; Wu, Lu, and Kang 2015). One study based on the 2012 CFPS data reported significant rural-urban differences in the prevalence of depressive symptoms for children aged 10 to 15 (14 percent vs. 24 percent for urban and rural children) (Zhou et al. 2018). The mental health status of left-behind children has been the subject of many studies in China, with most revealing serious mental health deficits for rural left-behind children lacking parental supervision (Gao 2008; Huang and Li 2007; Wu et al. 2015; Zhang et al. 2011). Migrant children in urban areas have been found to lag behind local urban children in subjective well-being, social anxiety, and loneliness (Hu et al. 2008; Wang and Zou 2010).

In this chapter, we describe and analyze the psychological well-being and social well-being of children between the ages of 10 and 15 based on questions and scales used in the CFPS. As we have done in previous chapters, we undertake our analyses with special attention to rural-urban disparities, gender differences, and variance based on different types of family living arrangements.

For psychological well-being, we examine psychological distress, sense of happiness, confidence in the future, self-esteem, and self-efficacy. The composite index of psychological distress comes from the adapted Chinese version of the Kessler Screening Scale for Psychological Distress (K6) screening tool (Kessler et al. 2002; Kessler et al. 2010). It consists of six questions asking respondents how often they experienced each of six symptoms of psychological distress and generalized anxiety disorder in the past month. In this study, psychological distress in the 2014 CFPS data is indicated when the child reports that he/she experiences any of the six symptoms "often" or "nearly every day."[1]

CFPS captures the respondents' states of happiness and confidence in the future using single questions asking the respondents how happy they feel and how confident they are in their future (Abdel-Khalek 2006). Children who report a score of seven or above on a ten-point scale from very unhappy ("0") to very happy ("10") or no confidence at all ("0") to very confident ("10") are regarded to be "happy" or "confident in their future."[2]

Self-esteem is measured using the Chinese version of the Rosenberg Self-Esteem Scale in CFPS. Each child's total score is the sum of scores for each of nine statements (Rosenberg, 1979).[3] Higher scores indicate higher self-esteem.[4] Self-efficacy, as defined by Bandura (1989), is the confidence that individuals have in their ability to organize and execute courses of action required to attain specific performance outcomes. CFPS used the first four items of the seven-item Pearlin Mastery Scale designed to measure the perception of individuals for their ability to control forces that significantly impact their lives (Pearlin and Schooler 1978). We summed the four items to get the self-efficacy score, with higher scores indicating higher self-efficacy.[5]

It is worth noting that self-esteem and self-efficacy are two related yet distinct self-constructs (Chen, Gully, and Eden 2004). Self-esteem refers to the general sense of self-worth, and self-efficacy refers to the sense of one's ability to achieve one's goals. People with high levels of self-esteem and self-efficacy are more likely to persist in the face of challenges and make great efforts in performing difficult tasks. Those with low self-esteem and self-efficacy often lack the confidence to take on challenging tasks and tend to avoid and procrastinate when faced with difficult and rewarding goals (Hajloo, 2014). Both are major factors related to individual psychological well-being and happiness.

For social well-being, we look at the children's self-evaluated inter-personal relations and their social skills. We utilize two indicators based on responses to two single questions asked of children aged 10–15. The respondents are asked to assess their inter-personal relations and their social skills on an 11-point continuous scale from 0 to 10, with 0 representing "very bad" and 10 representing "very good." Children who report a score of 7 or above on each of the two scales are regarded as having good inter-personal relations and social skills.[6]

Rural-urban disparities in child psychological and social well-being

We first look at child psychological and social well-being from the perspective of rural-urban disparities. Because different scales or response categories were adopted in the 2010 and 2014 waves of CFPS and thus the data for 2010 and 2014 are not directly comparable, we focus on the 2014 data in this section.

A quick glance at Figure 5.1 shows clear disparities in psychological and social well-being between rural and urban children as of 2014. Rural children are more likely to suffer psychological distress, report

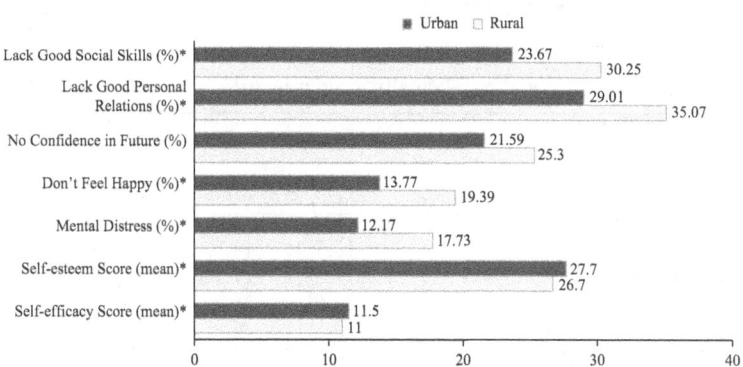

Figure 5.1 Selected variables on psychological and social well-being of children, 2014

Note: * $p < .05$ based on design-based Pearson chi-square statistic.

Significance level indicates the rural-urban difference in each variable.

feeling unhappy and less confident in their future. They also have lower self-esteem and self-efficacy scores than urban children. Socially, children in rural areas are significantly less likely to report having good personal relations or possessing good social skills.

Gender differences in child psychological and social well-being

Gender differences in mental health conditions such as depression and anxiety for children and adolescents in the US and European countries have been documented in many studies (Thapar et al. 2012; Weller et al. 2006). Adolescent girls, especially those after puberty, have been shown to experience more psychological complications than boys (Freire and Ferreira 2018; Weller et al. 2006). Adolescent girls also have a lower level of life satisfaction and overall subjective well-being than boys (Bradshaw et al. 2013; Kaye-Tzdok et al. 2017). In this section, we will examine how boys and girls in China differ in their psychological and social health indicators.

There are clear gender differences in social and emotional well-being among both rural and urban children. Table 5.1 shows that girls in both urban and rural areas report higher levels of nearly all indicators of social and emotional well-being than their male counterparts. Moreover, the compounded effects of gender and urban-rural community status make rural boys the most vulnerable of the four groups. For example, while only 9 percent of urban girls feel unhappy, more than 22 percent of rural boys report being unhappy. While 20 percent of urban girls report

Table 5.1 Social emotional well-being by gender in 2014

Variables	Rural		Urban	
	Female	Male	Female	Male
Mental distress (%)*	16.5	18.8	10.8	13.3
Don't feel happy (%)*	17.0	21.5	8.5	18.3
No confidence in future (%)*	23.6	26.7	17.1	25.4
Lack good personal relations (%)*	33.1	36.7	28.5	29.4
Lack good social skill (%)*	26.6	33.3	19.9	26.9
Self-esteem score (mean)*	26.6	26.7	27.9	27.5
Self-efficacy score (mean)*	11.1	10.9	11.4	11.6

Note: The sample sizes are $N=3,426$ for first five variables and $N=1,356$ for last two variables. * $p < .05$ based on design-based Pearson chi-square statistic indicates significant differences in values between at least two of four categories of children.

a lack of good social skills, a third of the rural boys do so. Contrary to findings of prior studies about gender difference in subjective well-being in western countries that favored boys (e.g., Kaye-Tzdok et al. 2017), our finding reveals a clear advantage for girls, especially in urban communities. In fact, urban girls have the highest level psychological and social level well-being in six of the seven indicators. They corroborate findings of earlier studies that urban girls have enjoyed unprecedented parental support and equal educational opportunities (Tsui and Rich 2002). In future research, it is important to examine the specific social and cultural environments that affect the subjective well-being of boys and girls.

Psychological and social well-being for children in different living arrangements

Children in different living arrangements tend to differ in levels of psychological and social well-being. The findings shown in Tables 5.2 and 5.3 indicate that children with both parents absent and single-parent or orphaned children are the two groups most vulnerable to psychological illness and social difficulties. In both 2010 and 2014, among all groups of children, single-parent and orphaned children are the most likely to experience mental distress and feeling of unhappiness and report a lack of social skills. In 2010, children left behind by both parents also fare much worse than children in intact families or left-behind children with one parent at home, with respect to level of happiness, confidence about their future, and social relations. Specifically, over a third of children who are left behind by both parents report having no confidence in their future and lacking good personal relations, much higher than any other groups of children. Similarly, for 2014, left-behind children with both parents absent also have lower levels of confidence in the future and social skills although the difference does not reach statistical significance.

On the other hand, in contrast to the plight of left-behind children with both parents absent, children with only one migrant parent are doing just as well as, if not better than, children of rural intact families in their psychological and social well-being. The above analysis indicates that migration of both parents, especially the mother (as most of the children left behind by one parent are left behind by their fathers), has an adverse effect on the social-emotional well-being of children, just like that of parental separation or death on single-parent/orphaned children.

Despite the many difficulties facing migrant children and their families in urban areas, they fare better in several psychological and social indicators than both rural left-behind children and rural children of

Table 5.2 Children's psychological and social well-being by family structure (%), 2010

Variables	Rural intact	Urban intact	LBC-no parent	LBC-1 parent	Migrant	Single-parent/orphan
Mental distress†	18.8	24.6	23.2	20.1	18.1	30.2
Don't feel happy*	20.2	17.7	27.8	14.4	16.1	30.3
No confidence in future*	20.9	18.6	33.6	20.3	24.1	27.8
Lack good personal relations*	33.3	23.0	38.9	29.7	22.8	36.7
Lack good social skill	26.2	22.1	30.6	25.0	20.2	31.7

Note: † .05< p < .10, * p < .05 based on design-based Pearson chi-square statistic.
The sample sizes are N=3,426 and 2,530 for 2010 and 2014.

Table 5.3 Children's psychological and social well-being by family structure (%), 2014

Variables	Rural intact	Urban intact	LBC-no parent	LBC-1 parent	Migrant	Single-parent/orphan
Mental distress†	16.9	10.3	16.2	19.0	17.3	22.8
Don't feel happy*	17.3	11.5	21.3	19.7	21.5	30.4
No confidence in future	25.0	19.7	27.7	24.7	23.8	28.3
Lack good personal relations	34.4	30.0	32.9	32.6	29.7	37.7
Lack good social skill	29.4	23.3	33.1	26.5	23.2	35.6

Note: † .05< p < .10, * p < .05 based on design-based Pearson chi-square statistic.
The sample sizes are N=3,426 and 2,530 for 2010 and 2014.

intact families, especially in 2010. For example, migrant children have higher levels of social well-being (good personal relationship and social skills) than all rural children in both 2010 and 2014.

As these indicators have different scales or response categories in the 2010 and 2014 surveys, they are not directly comparable across years. However, we may gain insight into the changes in the relative psychological and social well-being for children of different family structures. While the numbers in Table 5.3 reveal similar dire conditions in 2014 for single-parent and orphaned children, the well-being of children

Table 5.4 Self-esteem and self-efficacy for children in various living arrangements in 2010 and 2014

Variables	Rural intact	Urban intact	LBC-no parent	LBC-1 parent	Migrant	Single-parent/orphan
Year 2010						
Self-esteem score	25.47	26.93	25.56	25.08	25.88	26.05
Sig.	(a)	(a, b, c)	(b)	(c)		
Self-efficacy score	11.05	11.51	10.46	10.69	10.84	10.23
Sig.	(a, b, c)	(a, d, e, f, g)	(b, d)	(e)	(f)	(c, g)
Year 2014						
Self-esteem score	26.78	27.53	26.96	26.61	28.74	26.58
Sig.	(a, b)	(a, c, d)	(e)	(c, f)	(b, e, f, g)	(d, g)
Self-efficacy score	11.05	11.51	11.14	10.90	11.23	10.80
Sig.	(a)	(a, b, c, d)	(b)	(c)		(d)

Note: The sample sizes are $N=410$ (for 10-year-old children) in 2010 and 1,350 (10 to 14 years old) in 2014. For each variable in each year, the categories with the same subscripted letters are significantly different at $p < 0.05$ level. Variables are not comparable across years.

left-behind by both parents seem to have improved relative to other groups of children, compared to 2010. They no longer differ significantly from children in rural intact families or children left-behind by one parent in several indicators. This narrowing gap in well-being are in line with our earlier findings that both the family living conditions and the health status of children left behind by both parents have greatly improved from 2010 to 2014. Despite this, the general advantage of children in urban intact families over the other groups of children, including the left-behind children, is still substantial.

In Table 5.4 are shown the self-esteem and self-efficacy scores for children in different family structures. In both 2010 and 2014, we see that children in urban intact families have significantly higher levels of self-esteem and self-efficacy than children in rural intact families and the left-behind children. In 2014, migrant children have the highest mean self-esteem scores among children of different family structures, even higher than that of urban intact children.

Summary and discussion

Social and emotional developments are major components of life functioning and well-being of children (Darling-Churchill and Lippman

2012). The results presented in this chapter demonstrate that there are significant variations between rural and urban children in their social and emotional well-being. In particular, rural boys have clear social and emotional deficits compared to urban girls. Considering the traditional values of gender bias against girls in China, the high level of social and emotional well-being for girls needs further examination in future research.

Although some studies (e.g., Ren and Treiman 2016; Wen et al. 2015) found no significant impact of different family arrangements on the emotional well-being of children, we find there is consistent evidence for the psychological toll of parental absence on children due to internal migration, marital dissolution or death. Our findings demonstrate that children in single-parent families or children left behind by both parents are especially vulnerable to social and emotional challenges. Taking into consideration findings in earlier chapters, the picture that emerges is that well-being in multiple domains tend to go together.

Our findings about emotional deficits for different groups of children, including rural children in general, children left behind by both parents, and single-parent or orphaned children, suggest the need for further examination of family functioning and parent-child relationship in different family structures. It also spells out the urgent need for the adoption of effective intervention strategies targeting these emotionally vulnerable children and their families.

Notes

1 The corresponding response categories for the K6 questions in 2010 survey are "2 or 3 times per week" or "nearly every day."
2 The 2010 CFPS survey used a five-point scale of 1 ("very unhappy/no confidence at all") to 5 ("very happy/very confident") for the two questions "feel happy" and "confidence in the future." Respondents with a score of 4 and 5 are counted as being "happy" and "confident in the future."
3 One statement, "I wish I could have more respect for myself," is excluded from the original ten because of the inaccurate translation in the Chinese version.
4 The composite self-esteem scale has an unadjusted mean of 25.78 (sd = 2.24, min. = 19, max. = 35) in the 2014 CFPS survey.
5 Three items are reverse coded. The composition self-efficacy scale has an unadjusted mean of 10.96 (sd = 1.38, min. = 6, max. = 15) in the 2014 CFPS survey.
6 The 2010 CFPS survey used a five-point scale of 1 ("very poor") to 5 ("very good") for the two questions on personal relationships and social skills. Respondents with a score of 4 and 5 are counted as having "good" personal relationship and social skills.

6 Cognitive development and educational attainments

As the Chinese economy has grown, so has Chinese investment in education. Figure 6.1. plots China's school enrollment ratios and shows the progress China has made in improving access to education.

One of the oft-reported developments in China is the stellar performance of Chinese students in the PISA (Program in International Student Achievement) and in international competitions such as the International Mathematical Olympiad. While such performances inspire admiration and awe and add to argument of superior Chinese performance in math (Geary et al. 1993), they have also provoked reflection and self-criticism within China (Tan 2017). Most importantly, because these performances only capture the abilities of elite students and the PISA includes a relatively small number of provincial units, the stellar performances detract from the much more mixed picture of student cognitive and educational attainment. In a recent study, Khor et al. (2016) go as far as to argue that China may be facing a looming human capital crisis because of problems with secondary education and the need for a better educated labor force as the country seeks to move up the ladder of economic development.

Based on the CFPS data, this chapter describes the educational and cognitive well-being of China's children and youth. We define the cognitive and educational well-being of children and youths as their ability to learn language, mathematics, and other knowledge appropriate for their age levels. It includes their development of cognitive skills required to effectively understand their environment and to communicate with people.

Besides the family, child care centers, kindergartens, and schools are the major formal settings where children learn new knowledge and master various cognitive skills. It has been established that education at high-quality child care centers, pre-schools, and elementary schools are crucial for children's later educational achievement, personality skills,

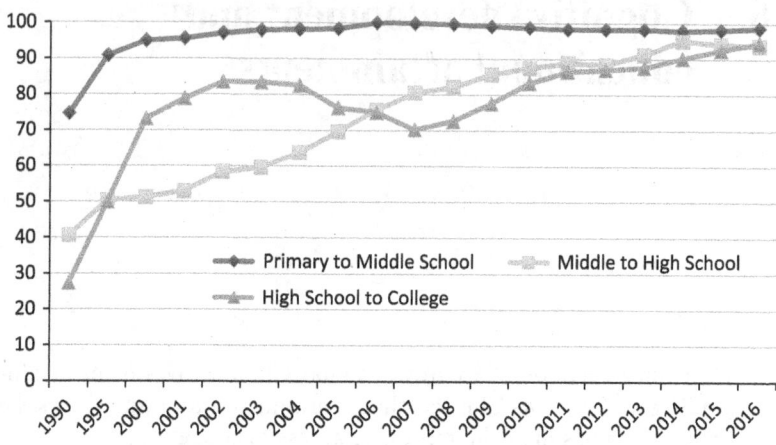

Figure 6.1 School enrollment ratios in China, 1990–2016

Note: Enrollment ratio from high school to college is the ratio of the total number of new college entrants to the number of graduates of academic high schools (excluding vocational high schools).

Source: Ministry of Education of China (2017b).

and future economic success (Duncan and Magnuson 2013; Heckman, Pinto, and Savelyev 2013; Reynolds et al. 2011).

We present data on enrollment in kindergartens and schools and compare the levels of school engagement, school satisfaction, and school performance between rural and urban children. We also look at variations in student aspirations for college as well as performance on math and vocabulary tests.

Kindergarten and school enrollment and college aspirations

Table 6.1 shows the distribution of child schooling in rural and urban China by age group. As of 2014, 67.5 percent of three to five year olds were in kindergarten, a significant increase of 12.7 percentage points from 2010.[1] Most of the increase can be attributed to a jump of nearly 16 percentage points in the proportion of rural children in preschool or kindergarten. This reflects both growing demand for pre-school education and the effectiveness of recent government efforts to promote such education in rural areas. However, the urban-rural disparity of more than 15 percentage points remains stark even if we didn't take

Table 6.1.1 School enrollment and college aspirations (%), 2014

Variables	Community type		Total
	Rural	Urban	
In kindergarten (age 3–5)*	63.3	78.8	67.5
In school (age 6–15) †	95.4	97.6	96.1
In boarding school (age 10–15)*	36.6	11.1	28.5
Aspire for college degree (age 10–15)*	58.8	85.4	66.8

Note: Sample size varies according to age group. Results weighted.
* $p < .05$ based on design-based Pearson chi-square statistic.

Table 6.1.2 Changes in school enrollment and college aspirations (percentage points), 2010 to 2014

Variables	Community type		Total
	Rural	Urban	
In kindergarten (age 3–5)	+15.8*	+2.6	+12.7
In school (age 6–15)	+3.4	+3.4	+3.4
In boarding school (age 10–15)	+5.9†	+3.6	+4.4
Aspire for college degree (age 10–15)	–0.0	+8.4*	+2.9

Note: Sample size varies according to age group.
† $.01 < p < .05$, * $p < .05$ based on design-based Pearson chi-square statistic.

into account quality differences between urban and rural pre-school education facilities.

Among children of compulsory education age (6 to 15), 98 percent in urban and 95 percent in rural areas were enrolled in school in 2014, a modest but noticeable increase from 2010. These numbers point to China's continuing progress in universalizing nine years of compulsory education in both urban and rural areas.

Among 10–15 year olds, the numbers for boarding school enrollment stand out. 37 percent of rural children and 11 percent of urban children in 2014 lived in school dormitories, compared to 31 percent and 8 percent, respectively, in 2010. These are very high numbers and, as we noted in Chapter 2, are mainly the consequence of the government's school consolidation polices that greatly reduced the number of schools and increased the distances students have to travel to school.

For the same 10–15 age group, more than 85 percent of the urbanites vs. 59 percent of those with rural *hukou* aspire to go to college (2014).

Remarkably, the percentage of urban students who aspire to college increased by more than 8 percentage points between 2010 and 2014 but the proportion of rural students aspiring for college remains at 58 percent. The relative diminishment of rural aspirations for higher education may be due to a variety of factors but it appears the school consolidation may be a contributing factor.

Table 6.2.1 shows children's schooling status and college aspirations by living arrangements. Between 2010 and 2014, kindergarten enrollment increased substantially for all groups of children, especially left-behind children, except for children in urban intact families. Left-behind

Table 6.2.1 School enrollment and college aspirations by living arrangement (%), 2014

Variables	Rural intact	Urban intact	LBC-no parent	LBC-1 parent	Migrant	Single-parent/ orphan
In kindergarten (age 3–5)*	63.4	79.2	64.3	61.4	77.4	68.8
In school (age 6–15)	95.6	97.5	96.1	97.1	96.5	93.4
In boarding school (age 10–15)*	37.5	11.1	34.8	35.0	7.3	29.1
Aspire for college degree (age 10–15)*	60.6	86.1	63.7	59.8	84.2	54.6

Note: Sample size varies according to age group. Results weighted. * $p < .05$ based on design-based Pearson chi-square statistic.

Table 6.2.2 School enrollment and college aspirations by living arrangement (%), 2010

Variables	Rural intact	Urban intact	LBC: no parent	LBC: 1 parent	Migrant	Single-parent/ orphan
In kindergarten (age 3–5) *	50.3	79.8	43.7	49.0	61.9	56.4
In school (age 6–15)	92.6	94.7	91.6	92.9	90.9	89.2
In boarding school (age 10–15) *	31.8	7.8	29.4	22.8	13.6	17.3
Aspire for college degree (age 10–15) *	60.3	78.7	57.2	62.6	69.0	53.8

Note: Sample size varies according to age group. Results weighted. * $p < .05$ based on design-based Pearson chi-square statistic.

children with no parents at home had the lowest proportion of kindergarten enrollment (44 percent) in 2010 but caught up with those in rural intact families in 2014.

For school enrolment, school-aged children in different living arrangements all achieved 90 percent-plus school enrollment rates, ranging from 93 percent for children with a single parent or orphaned to 97 percent for children of urban intact families. As noted earlier, for students aged 10–15, the proportion of school boarders further increased for children in different living arrangements except for migrant children. More than one-third of the students in rural intact families and left-behind children lived in school dormitories.

Disaggregation of student aspirations for a college degree reveals some striking patterns. Children of urban intact families, migrant children, and left-behind children with no parent present increased their college aspirations from 2010 to 2014, though absolute level of aspirations for the last category (LBC-no parent) remained low. Most interestingly, 84 percent of the migrant children had college ambitions, nearly the same as their urban counterparts. These internal migrants are evidently China's strivers. This shows that *hukou* status was not the determining factor for college aspirations as far as these two groups were concerned even though there exists a large urban-rural gap in children's college aspirations overall.

Class size in primary and middle schools

Having reported on enrollment and before we examine the data on student satisfaction with their school, we take a look at class size, which we expected to have been affected by trends discussed in Chapter 2, particularly the official push for school consolidation. With the closure of schools in outlying areas and the concentration of students in the centrally located schools, overcrowded urban schools (and dormitories) have become the norm. According to a 2011 government report, most schools with large class sizes (56 or more students) are concentrated in county seats (towns)[2] (县城) and cities, especially the former (Wang 2011).

The class sizes as reported by children in the CFPS survey are similar for 2010 and 2014 and we report only the 2014 figures in Table 6.3. While the urban class sizes were at or above 50 for all ages (10–15), the rural class sizes were under the standard size of 45 for 10 and 11 year olds, increasing gradually to 49 and 50 for 13 to 15 year olds. This appears to be due to rural children moving from community primary schools to centralized middle schools. The higher standard deviations for the rural class sizes

Table 6.3 Reported class size in rural and urban areas (age 10–15), 2014

Child Age	Rural		Urban	
	Mean	SD	Mean	SD
Age 10*	43	17	55	12
Age 11*	43	16	51	12
Age 12*	46	16	51	12
Age 13*	49	15	52	10
Age 14	50	15	52	12
Age 15	49	14	50	12

Note: Sample size $N=2,379$, including all 10- to 15-year-old children who are in school. Results are weighted. * Indicates significant urban-rural differences in the mean score at $p < .05$.

indicate greater variation. For 10-year-old rural children, 36 percent of them have classes either below 24 or above 60 (i.e., 17 above or below the mean). Looking regionally, the western region, compared to the coastal and central regions, stood out in that its urban children had the largest average class size of 55 whereas its rural children had the smallest class size of 44, a pattern that Wang (2011) reported for earlier periods.

The large class sizes in China exceed the government-required standard and the class size restrictions of developed countries and are known to exert an adverse effect on the quality of education (Ma, 2009). In 2016, the Chinese government issued a set of guidelines for promoting the integrated development of compulsory education in counties. To address the issue of overcrowded classes, local authorities were encouraged to invest in building new or expanding existing schools, developing rural community schools, and hiring more qualified teachers (State Council 2016a).

School satisfaction, study engagement, and performance

Having looked at school enrollment and class sizes, we now look at the students' school experiences and performance. The data on study engagement are based on the average score of five items asking students about their study habits on a five-point Likert scale that ranges from "strongly disagree (1)" to "strongly agree (5)": "study hard," "pay attention to study in class," "double check homework after completion to guarantee correctness," "obey school rules and disciplines," and "don't play until completing homework." School satisfaction is measured by the average score of five items asking each student about his/her satisfaction with school, head teacher, Chinese teacher, math teacher, and English teacher on a five-point Likert scale from "very dissatisfied (1)" to "very satisfied (5)." Satisfaction with study performance is measured by a single item ("How do you think of your academic performance?") on a scale from "very dissatisfied (1)" to "very satisfied (5)." Self-evaluation as a student is measured by the single item ("How good do you think you are as a student?") on a scale from "very bad (1)" to "excellent (5)."

Table 6.4 shows the mean scores of each category for the four indicators and the differences (changes) between 2010 and 2014. For

Table 6.4 Study engagement, school satisfaction, and self-reported performance for children aged 10–15, 2010 to 2014

Indicator	Community	Gender	Year 2010		Year 2014		2014 & 2010	
			Mean	Sig.	Mean	Sig.	Difference	Sig.
Study engagement								
	Rural	Female	3.68	ac	3.82	ac	0.15	*
	Rural	Male	3.49	ab	3.66	ab	0.17	*
	Urban	Female	3.68	bd	3.80	bd	0.12	*
	Urban	Male	3.53	cd	3.62	cd	0.09	
School satisfaction								
	Rural	Female	4.03	ac	4.19		0.16	*
	Rural	Male	3.96	abd	4.10		0.14	*
	Urban	Female	4.27	bce	4.20		−0.07	
	Urban	Male	4.08	de	4.09		0.00	
Satisfaction with academic performance								
	Rural	Female	3.41	a	3.40	a	−0.01	
	Rural	Male	3.22	ab	3.33		0.10	
	Urban	Female	3.42	b	3.41	b	−0.01	
	Urban	Male	3.32		3.22	ab	−0.10	
Self-evaluation as a student								
	Rural	Female	3.29	a	3.20	a	−0.09	
	Rural	Male	3.06	abc	3.12	b	0.06	
	Urban	Female	3.32	bc	3.29	bc	−0.03	
	Urban	Male	3.23	c	3.10	ac	−0.14	

Note: Sample sizes are 3,359 and 2,956 in 2010 and 2014. Results are weighted. Differences are rounded up from calculations preformed to the third decimal point.
For each category, * indicates that 2010 and 2014 scores for a group of children are significantly different at $p < .05$.
For each indicator of each year, scores of the groups with the same superscripted letters are significantly different at $p < 0.05$.

study engagement, there is no significant urban-rural difference—a pattern also observed in 2010—but there exist gender differences in favor of girls in terms of study engagement. Moreover, study engagement improved from 2010 to 2014 except for urban boys.

Regarding school satisfaction, rural students were clearly less satisfied with their schools in 2010 but that difference largely disappeared in 2014 as there was a significant increase in reported school satisfaction by rural students. The increase in reported rural student satisfaction with schools thus points to the possibility that school conditions and teaching quality in rural areas improved in the study period.[3]

We also looked at all four indicators by living arrangement but have omitted the accompanying table here for the sake of space. In contrast to 2010, there were in 2014 no longer significant differences between children in different living arrangements except for satisfaction with academic performance. Rural children and left-behind children were just as engaged with their studies and as satisfied with school as the urban intact children. In 2010, rural children left behind by both parents were less satisfied with their schools than either rural or urban children in intact families. In 2014, however, their school satisfaction scores had significantly increased so that they were just as satisfied with their schools as other children. Improvement in school conditions in rural areas appears to have especially benefited left-behind children, especially where increased school boarding put the left-behind children on a level playing field with the other students. Nonetheless, as in 2010, left-behind children with both parents away reported the lowest levels of satisfaction with their academic performance in 2014, especially when compared to rural students from intact families, who reported a significant increase from 2010. We shall delve further into the impact of parental absence in a later chapter.

Vocabulary and math test scores

We now look at students' cognitive abilities of the 10 to 15 year olds based on CFPS-administered tests on Chinese vocabulary and math. The vocabulary test is a test of language ability designed to measure recognition of Chinese characters and phrases. The math test is a test of children's math and computational skills based on levels of difficulty. The Chinese and mathematical questions are selected based on standard school curriculum and administered to each child starting on the question and character/phrase appropriate for that child's school grade level. The test scores are the number of questions that are correctly answered (Huang and Xie 2013).[4]

Table 6.5.1 Children's test scores, 2014

Type of test	Mean test score			
	Rural female	*Rural male*	*Urban female*	*Urban male*
Vocabulary test*	21.2[abc]	20.2[ade]	24.5[bdf]	23.3[cef]
Math test*	10.1[ab]	9.8[cd]	12.5[ac]	11.7[bd]

Note: Sample size $N=2,956$. Results weighted. The categories with the same superscripted letters are significantly different at $p < 0.05$ based on postestimation T test of means.

Table 6.5.2 Changes in children's test score (age 10–15), 2010 to 2014

Type of test	Difference in 2010 and 2014 test scores							
	Rural female	*Sig.*	*Rural male*	*Sig.*	*Urban female*	*Sig.*	*Urban male*	*Sig.*
Vocabulary test	–0.44		–0.04		–0.11		–0.44	
Math test	–0.90	*	–0.91	*	0.26		–0.76	

Note: * The score differences are significant at $p < 0.05$ based on postestimation T test of means.

Results from the 2014 battery of tests show that rural children, both male and female, continued to perform poorly relative to the urban children in both Chinese character recognition and math computation (Table 6.5.1). Rural males had the lowest average scores. Also noteworthy is that the 2014 average math scores for rural children dropped significantly from 2010 while the scores for urban females rose (Table 6.5.2).

Table 6.6 shows the test scores of children in different living arrangements for both 2010 and 2014 as well as the score differences between the 2010 and 2014 waves. Comparing the average test scores of 2010 and 2014, we find that the vocabulary test score for left-behind children with no parent at home increased while the scores of all the other groups decreased. The average math test scores for children in rural intact families and left-behind children with one parent dropped significantly between 2010 and 2014.

In both years, children in urban intact families generally performed better than all other groups except when compared with migrant children in the vocabulary test. Children from rural intact families are not

Table 6.6 Children's test scores by living arrangement (age 10–15), 2010 and 2014

Type of test	Living arrangement	Year 2010 Mean	Sig.	Year 2014 Mean	Sig.	Difference Means	Sig.
Vocabulary test							
	Rural intact	20.89	abc	20.78	ab	–0.12	
	Urban intact	23.98	adef	23.62	acd	–0.37	
	LBC-no parent	20.53	dg	21.82	e	1.30	
	LBC-1 parent	21.51	eh	20.71	cf	–0.80	
	Migrant children	24.25	bghi	24.23	bef	–0.02	
	Single-parent/orphan	22.17	cfi	20.82	d	–1.35	
Math test							
	Rural intact	10.91	a	10.04	ab	–0.87	*
	Urban intact	12.36	abcd	12.11	acde	–0.25	
	LBC-no parent	10.98	b	10.16	c	–0.81	
	LBC-1 parent	10.80	c	9.57	df	–1.23	*
	Migrant children	11.71		11.67	bf	–0.04	
	Single-parent/orphan	11.11	d	10.31	e	–0.80	

Note: Sample size $N=3,360$ in 2010 and 2,539 in 2014.
* indicates that the 2010 and 2014 scores for that group of children are significantly difference at $p <0.05$. For each indicator, the scores of groups with the same superscripted letters are significantly different at $p < 0.05$.

significantly different from the left-behind children with either one parent or no parent at home for both tests and in both years. Indeed, left-behind children with no parent at home had similar performance in both tests as left-behind children with one parent and rural intact children. It is worth noting the outstanding performance of migrant children, who had the highest vocabulary test scores, and the second highest math test scores.

High school and post-secondary enrollment

The nine-year compulsory education system in China covers six years of primary school and three years of middle school education. After completing middle school, students must take a competitive exam for admission to high school, including academic high schools and vocational high schools. The former is supposed to prepare students for post-secondary education while graduates of the vocational high schools go into the job market. According to the Ministry of Education, the ratio of middle school graduates who go to all types of high schools has increased from 87.5 percent in 2010 to 93.7 percent in 2016. This means that, as of 2016, more than 6 percent of China's middle school graduates did NOT go to any type of high school and most likely joined the labor force immediately. Because of significant provincial variations, the Ministry of Education has called on all provincial units to raise the middle to high school enrollment ratio to over 90 percent by 2020 (MOE 2017b).

Studies have shown that the children in poorer rural areas fail to go to or drop out of high school mainly because of the high costs (tuition and fees) as well as poor preparedness (Liu et al. 2009). In fact, in a survey of middle school students, Yi et al. (2012) found that many middle school students dropped out by the first month of grade 9, the last year of compulsory education, because of poverty and low expectations about more education owing to poor academic performance. The poor management and teaching quality of vocational or technical high schools intended to prepare rural adolescents for the industrial workforce also contributed to the high drop-out rate (Yi et al. 2015). With the end of the era of unlimited supply of labor in China, earnings for entry level workers have increased substantially and have thus raised the opportunity costs of staying in school, particularly for youths who see little opportunity of excelling in post-secondary institutions.

In this section, we describe the education status of youths aged 16 to 19 as of 2014. As Table 6.7 shows, the proportion of youths not in school increased rapidly with age because youths of these ages (and their families) had to make various difficult decisions about whether to compete for entry into high school (academic track or vocational track), to drop out of high school, and whether to attend college after high school. For readers who have followed our findings thus far, it should not surprise anyone that the pattern was stronger in rural areas. Yet they may still find the magnitude of urban-rural differences astounding. At age 16, 7 percent of urban youth and three times as many (21 percent) of the rural youth had already left school. At 19 years of age, 43 percent of the urban youths were in post-secondary institutions but only 19 percent of rural youth were. While most urban youth go on to post-secondary education after finishing high school, most rural children are done with their schooling before college (Li et al. 2015). These differences in schooling reflect not only differences in abilities but also variations in access to resources and aspirations, which government policies have served to perpetuate (Yi et al. 2015).

Table 6.7 Education status of 16–19 year olds by community type (%), 2014

School Level	Rural				Urban			
	Age 16	Age 17	Age 18	Age 19	Age 16	Age 17	Age 18	Age 19
Not in school	21	33	37	51	7	8	27	39
Middle school	36	13	3	1	23	4	1	0
High school	43	51	52	29	69	87	65	18
College	0	2	8	19	1	1	7	43
Total	100	100	100	100	100	100	100	100

Note: Sample size *N*=1,689. Results are weighted.

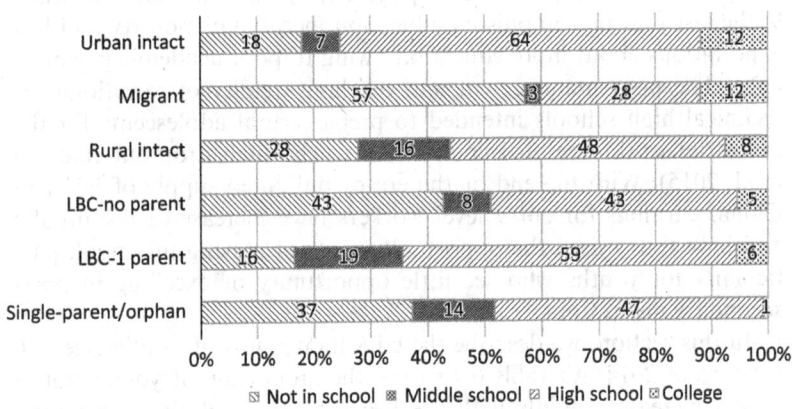

Figure 6.2 Educational status of youth aged 16–19 by living arrangement (%), 2014

Note: Sample size *N*=1,689. Results are weighted.

Figure 6.2 shows the percentage of youths in different school levels for each of the six types of living arrangements as of 2014. The urban-rural differences, discussed above, again show clearly, with rural intact youths having left school at 28 percent, 10 percentage points higher than for youths in urban intact families. Compared to rural and urban intact family youths, a much higher proportion of youth left behind by both parents (43 percent) or with deceased or divorced parents (37 percent) are not in school. Surprisingly, more than half of migrant youths are not in school, although a higher proportion of migrant youth than any other group of rural youth are in college.[5]

We also looked into the distribution of age and school levels for rural children in eastern, central, and western regions but have omitted the accompanying figure for the sake of space. In general, school attendance patterns were similar in eastern and central China, but youths in the western region entered a school grade level later and left school earlier. For instance, at age 16, half of rural youths in the western region still attended middle school, compared with only 32 percent in the eastern region and 22 percent in the central region. At age 19, nearly two-thirds of the rural youths in the western region were out of school and only 12 percent attended college. In contrast, over 20 percent of the 19 year olds in the eastern and central regions attend college and less than half had left school.

Summary and conclusion

Over the past two decades Chinese education has expanded alongside the Chinese economy. Yet the general picture of growth obscures the many variations and complexities in the Chinese education system. In our description and analysis of the educational and cognitive well-being of China's children and youth, we have looked at a broad array of elements and factors, including school enrollment, class size, reported satisfaction with school and with one's academic performance, the scores of their tests on vocabulary and math, their college aspirations, and educational attainment. We have given special attention to urban-rural differences as well as variations based on age, gender, family structure, and region.

Given the many factors and variations involved, we would like to highlight a number of developments here. A comparison of child educational well-being between 2010 and 2014 shows large increases in the proportion of rural children, including left-behind children, who were enrolled in pre-school and reported a high level of satisfaction with schools. Despite this, there still exist significant differences between rural and urban children in pre-school education, high school attendance, and college aspirations. The rural-urban gap is clearly seen in the lower cognitive test scores for rural children. Efforts by the Chinese government and non-government entities to boost school quality and access in less-developed areas are welcome but far from adequate.

Given the huge concerns about left-behind children and youth and migrant children, it is especially interesting to note that migrant children's performance in cognitive tests match that of urban children and is much better than all other rural children. Migrant youth aged 16 to 18 fare just as well as urban youth in college attendance. They are China's strivers.

Notes

1 In China, kindergartens are for children aged three to six before they start the nine-year compulsory formal schooling. Kindergarten is not part of the compulsory education. Although some kindergartens are funded and managed by local governments, most are privately owned and operated.
2 The towns that serve as county seats are usually the most populous and industrialized towns in the county with a large concentration of residents with urban hukou.
3 Achievement of equity in the public education system between rural and urban areas and between urban children and migrant children has been a major goal in the "National Plan for Medium- and Long-Term Education Reform and Development (2010 to 2020)." The central government has designed detailed standards to assess local government efforts in promoting education equity through allocation of more educational resources (i.e., facilities and teaching) in rural schools, enrollment of migrant children in local public schools, and establishment of system of care for left-behind children (See, MOE 2012). By the end of 2017, 81 percent of the counties in China, including all counties of 11 provinces, had passed the national assessment process (MOE 2017a).
4 See Huang and Xie (2013) for a detailed explanation of the contents and administration of the cognitive tests.
5 A major reason for the high proportion of migrant youth not in school is that they have difficulty enrolling in public high schools in urban areas because of policy barriers as noted in Chapter 2.

7 Community and family

Theories and research on human development have put great emphasis on the importance of various contexts and their relationship on child development (e.g., Bronfenbrenner 1979). In previous chapters, we examined the developmental well-being of children in different domains. In this chapter, we describe and analyze the multiple contexts of child development, especially the influence of families and communities.

The family is the most basic setting in which children are raised and educated. It is established that parental investment in a stimulating home environment, and the maintenance of appropriate parenting and nurturing relationship with children are crucial for children's early development of physical growth, cognitive capability, and social skills (Henrich and Gadaire 2008; Linver, Brooks-Gunn, and Kohen 2002; Shonkoff and Phillips 2000; Yeung, Linver, and Brooks-Gunn 2008). Positive parenting behaviors are found to benefit social-emotional and cognitive development of toddlers (Li and Xie 2017). With its Confucian tradition and in spite of the Chinese Communist revolution, the importance of the family in China has remained (Eastman 1989; Faure 2007) and family functioning is thus at least equally critical for child development in China as in developed economies. More generally, Chinese parents tend to be "quite warm and authoritative toward their children, with their love and care particularly being manifest in their efforts to ensure and promote their children's physical and material well-being (Wang and Chang 2010)."

Meanwhile, neighborhood and community contexts also exert significant influence on child development (Putnam 2015; Sampson 2003). It is recognized that China's collectivist culture impacts children's individual socioemotional adjustment (Chen 2000). Community poverty levels, safety, neighbor relations, access to high-quality child care facilities and schools, and availability of other social services are all factors that impact child development (Brooks-Gunn 1997; Diez Roux 2001; Luster and Okagaki 2006).

All too often, community contexts both affect and interact with family dynamics to impact child development. While unfavorable material conditions hinder children's growth in poor areas, some scholars propose that these children's cognitive delays may also be linked with lack of appropriate parenting practices (Yue et al. 2017). Parents and caregivers in rural China, who tend to be less educated than their counterparts in metropolitan centers, are more likely to engage in authoritarian parenting styles and tend to refrain from interactive practices such as storytelling or playing, leading to disadvantageous developmental outcomes such as delays in the development of social-emotional, cognitive, and language skills (Luo et al. 2017).

This chapter draws on the CFPS data to describe and examine Chinese children's family and community contexts. We begin with an overview of community and neighborhood contexts by looking at community level physical and social venues where children interact and socialize with others. The rest of the chapter is given to the description and analysis of family structure, home environment, parenting styles, caregivers' attitudes on parental responsibilities, and parental engagement and interaction with children.

Community context

Harking back to the first chapters, we first provide an overview of community and neighborhood contexts, which exert major influences on child well-being and development. Aspects of neighborhood context include community income/poverty level, safety, neighbor relations, access to child care facilities and schools, and availability of other social services.

In discussing community conditions, the most striking pattern that stares at us is the urban-rural contrast (Table 7.1). Based on simple indicators as reported by community administrators or observed by interviewers, the economic and living conditions of rural communities were and still are much poorer than those in urban communities. Almost all urban children lived in communities with tap water and clean cooking fuel, compared to just over half of the rural children. Urban communities also had more public service institutions or facilities—such as pharmacies, sportsgrounds, or playgrounds—than urban communities. 84 percent of urban children had access to a kindergarten in their community compared to only 51 percent of rural children though a similar percentage of rural children and urban

Table 7.1 Children's community conditions by community type, 2010 to 2014

Community conditions	Year 2010		Year 2014		2010 to 2014	
	Percentage or mean score	Sig.	Percentage or mean score	Sig.	Difference	Sig.
Tap water as main drinking water source						
Rural	39%	*	53%	*	14%	*
Urban	94%		98%		4%	
Gas/solar/methane as primary cooking fuel						
Rural	38%	*	57%	*	19%	*
Urban	91%		94%		3%	
Kindergarten in premise						
Rural	45%	*	51%	*	6%	
Urban	80%		84%		4%	
Primary school in community						
Rural	71%	*	63%		−8%	
Urban	55%		60%		5%	
Observed economic conditions by interviewer						
Rural	3.89	*	4.43	*	0.55	*
Urban	4.63		5.31		0.68	*
Street cleanliness observed by interviewer						
Rural	4.19	*	4.51	*	0.33	
Urban	4.95		5.22		0.26	
Number of public service institution/facilities (<=8)						
Rural	3.36	*	3.54	*	0.18	
Urban	4.79		5.15		0.35	

Note: All children with community information are included, with $N=8,880$ in 2010 and $N=7,497$ in 2014.
* $p <.05$ based on design-based Pearson chi-square statistic.
* in columns 3 and 5 indicates significant rural-urban differences, and in the last column significant 2014 and 2010 differences.

children (63 percent and 60 percent) had a primary school in their community.

Yet it should be underscored that, despite their obvious disadvantages, rural communities have nonetheless improved significantly since 2010. Rural access to tap water and clean cooking fuel increased by 14 and 19 percentage points respectively from 2010 to 2014. The number of rural communities with a kindergarten also increased by 6 percentage points. However, it is worth noting that the number of rural communities with primary schools declined substantially (71 percent to 63 percent) as a result of the school consolidation campaign discussed earlier.

Neighborhood and relative relationships

The CFPS includes several questions about whether and how each family interacted with their neighbors and relatives in various ways "during the last month" (i.e., very harmonious, harmonious, so-so, tense). Because of changes in the questions included between 2010 and 2014, we have only included the table using data from CFPS 2014 (Table 7.2).[1] In terms of relations with neighbors, there were no significant differences between rural and urban intact families (see Table 7.2). Families in the other types of living arrangements, especially left-behind children with one parent at home and migrant families, scored somewhat lower on this indicator. These variations point to the social cost those families had to bear as they strove to better their fortunes.

For the relationship with relatives, only 5 percentage points separate the lowest scoring from the highest scoring, suggesting that Chinese families in different types of living arrangements perceive they were relatively even in maintaining contacts with relatives. Not surprisingly, rural intact families, who would have had less difficulty in sustaining social relations based on kinship, scored the highest while families of single-parent/orphaned children reported the least close contact. Left-behind children with no parent also reported much less "close contact with relatives." In rural communities in China where an extended network of relatives forms an important social and economic safety net for

Table 7.2 Family relations with neighbors and relatives, 2014

Living arrangement	Good relations with neighbors		Close contact with relatives	
	Percent (%)	Sig.	Percent (%)	Sig.
Rural intact	72.2		60.2	a
Urban intact	73.7	ab	56.2	
LBC-no parent	68.3		55.3	
LBC-1 parent	65.4	a	57.3	
Migrant	66.0	b	57.0	
Single-parent/orphan	68.4		50.3	a

Note: Sample size is 8,262 in 2014. Results are weighted.
For each indicator, the scores of child groups with the same superscripted letters are significantly different at $p < 0.05$.

families, the reduction in close contact with relatives means a decrease in social capital and thus put single-parent and orphaned children and left-behind children with no parent at home at a social disadvantage.

Family structure

While the traditional family structure of two married individuals with their offspring has increasingly ceded space to alternative forms of family and partnerships in the US and other developed economies, the traditional family structure remains dominant in China even while most families have had to comply with the national family planning policies. Nonetheless, as we have shown in Table 1.1, the family structure profile in contemporary China bears unmistakably the hallmarks of a society and economy undergoing enormous and imbalanced growth. Tens of millions of adults have migrated across regions for job opportunities and yet are still bound by the *hukou* system. Data from CFPS 2010 showed that 13 percent of Chinese children did not live with their parents and another 15 percent lived with only one parent at home. The left-behind children with no parent at home—often left in the care of grandparents who tend to be less educated and in frail health—are especially at a developmental disadvantage.

Children of single parents (often due to divorce) or who are orphaned account for 4.5 percent of the child population and are in a similar situation. In addition to the deficit of parental care, they also suffer from the psychological trauma of parental separation or early parental death (Dong, Wang, and Ollendick 2002; Liu et al. 2000; Maier and Lachman 2000). In the previous chapters, we have documented the adverse effect of parental absence due to migration or marital dissolution on various domains of child development. We will further explore the impact of parental absence on child development outcomes in Chapters 9 and 10.

Observed home environment

CFPS interviewers were asked to observe whether there were pictorials, children's books, and other education materials in the child's home and whether the parents and caregivers actively communicated with the child. The observations of the interviewers are summarized in Table 7.3. In both 2010 and 2014, the urban-rural differences are clear. Children in urban intact families had the most stimulating home environments with books and education materials, and their parents or caregivers were most likely to communicate actively with them. Although we have learned in Chapter 3 that the living conditions of migrant children were not as good

Table 7.3 Observed home environment by living arrangement (age 0–15), 2010 to 2014

Observed Home environment	Year 2010 %	Sig.	Year 2014 %	Sig.	2010 to 2014 % Diff.	Sig.
Stimulating home environment*						
Rural intact	42.6	ab	61.8	ab	19.1	*
Urban intact	64.9	acdef	73.2	acde	8.2	*
LBC- no parent	39.2	cg	54.1	cf	14.8	*
LBC-1 parent	42.2	dh	58.3	dgh	16.1	*
Migrant	54.9	beghi	70.5	fgi	15.6	*
Single-parent/orphan	37.3	fi	49.6	behi	12.2	*
Parents communicate with child*						
Rural intact	55.0	abcd	70.0	ab	15.0	*
Urban intact	70.9	aefg	79.2	acde	8.2	*
LBC- no parent	42.4	behi	62.5	cf	20.1	*
LBC-1 parent	55.0	fhj	64.2	dg	9.2	*
Migrant	64.8	cik	75.8	fgh	11.0	
Single-parent/orphan	40.7	dgjk	57.9	beh	17.2	*

Note: Sample sizes are 8,987 and 7,353 in 2010 and 2014. Results are weighted.
For each indicator, the scores of child groups with same superscripted letters are significantly different at $p < 0.05$.
* indicates that the 2010 and 2014 scores for that group of children are significantly different at $p < 0.05$.

as those of their urban counterparts, migrant children also had more stimulating home environments than the left-behind children (LBC) or single-parent and orphaned children. This is further evidence that the migrant families are China's strivers. Single-parent and orphaned children have the least favorable home environments of all the groups.

Table 7.3 also demonstrates that, between 2010 and 2014, which were years of Chinese hyper-growth, the observed home environments improved significantly for nearly all child groups, especially for rural intact children and left-behind children. Even though the urban-rural disparity persisted, the proportion of children in rural intact families with a stimulating home environment increased by 19 percentage points, from 43 percent in 2010 to 62 percent in 2014.

Parental involvement in child's education

Family involvement in children's education, such as reading to children, paying attention to and helping with their homework, have been shown

Table 7.4 Caregiver involvement in child education in China, 2010 and 2014

Educational activity	Year 2010			Year 2014		
	Rural (%)	Urban (%)	sig.	Rural (%)	Urban (%)	sig.
Read to child (ages 3–5)	49.6	77.9	*	62.7	77.6	*
Buy child books (ages 3–5)	32.3	67.0	*	45.8	63.0	*
Supervise homework (ages 10–15)	79.0	86.4	*	82.2	81.8	
Offer homework tutoring (ages 10–15)	35.0	54.5	*	42.9	48.1	

Note: Sample sizes differ based on age group. * $p < .05$ based on design-based Pearson chi-square statistic.

to be effective in promoting child development and schooling (Fantuzzo et al. 2004; Luo et al. 2017). To understand parents' or other primary caregivers' involvement in their children's education, we use four indicators: reading to the child, buying books for the child, homework supervision, and tutoring.[2] Table 7.4 shows the percentages of rural and urban children whose parents or caregivers were actively involved in their education in 2010 and 2014. Among children three to five years old, a significantly higher proportion of urban parents acquired books and read stories to their children than parents or caregivers in rural areas. However, there was a significant increase in the involvement of rural parents and caregivers in the early education of their children in 2014. This development appeared to be prompted by the wider enrollment of rural children in nurseries and pre-schools, as we discussed in the previous chapter.

For children (ages 10–15) already in primary or middle schools, the rural-urban gap in parents' supervision and tutoring of children's homework, observed as significant in 2010, disappeared in 2014. In a clear indication of the generally high commitment of Chinese parents to educating their children, about 82 percent of parents were found to provide supervision of children's homework in 2014. Interestingly, while the percentage of urban parents who offer homework tutoring for their children actually dropped from 54 percent in 2010 to 48 percent in 2014, it rose from 35 to 43 percent for rural parents, thus bringing the two groups much closer together. This change may be due to a host of factors, including teaching qualities in urban vs. rural schools. One hypothesis is that urban parents increasingly recognized the importance

Table 7.5 Caregiver involvement in child education by living arrangement, 2010 and 2014

Educational activity	Year 2010 Percent %	Sig.	Year 2014 Percent %	Sig.	2014 and 2010 % Difference	Sig.
Reading to child (ages 3–5)						
Rural intact	55	abcd	66	ab	10.8	*
Urban intact	81	abefgh	81	acd	−0.8	
LBC-no parent	32	ceijk	45	bcef	13.4	*
LBC-1 parent	54	fil	59	d	5.0	
Migrant	67	dgjl	76	e	8.7	
Single-parent/orphan	61	hk	65	f	4.2	
Buying child books (ages 3–5)						
Rural intact	37	abc	50	ab	13.4	*
Urban intact	69	adefg	63	cd	−6.1	
LBC-no parent	21	bdhij	32	acef	10.6	
LBC-1 parent	37	ehk	40	bd	2.8	
Migrant	54	cfik	54	e	−0.9	
Single-parent/orphan	42	gj	58	f	16.1	
Supervise homework (ages 10–15)						
Rural intact	81	a	83	a	2.2	
Urban intact	87	abcd	85	b	−2.0	
LBC-no parent	72	b	79	c	6.8	
LBC-1 parent	76	ce	87	de	11.5	*
Migrant	85	e	64	abcd	−20.7	*
Single-parent/orphan	79	d	77	e	−2.1	
Homework tutoring (ages 10–15)						
Rural intact	38	abc	45	a	6.9	*
Urban intact	53	adef	50	b	−3.1	
LBC-no parent	26	bdgh	31	abc	4.6	
LBC-1 parent	34	ei	43		8.7	
Migrant	52	cgi	40		−11.6	
Single-parent/orphan	40	fh	46	c	6.5	

Note: Sample sizes are 8,990 and 7,353 in 2010 and 2014. Results are weighted.
* indicates that the 2010 and 2014 scores for that group of children are significantly difference at $p < 0.05$.
For each indicator, the scores of child groups with the same superscripted letters are significantly different at $p < 0.05$.

of children's autonomy while still maintaining a high standard and close supervision of children's schoolwork (Naftali 2009).

Table 7.5 shows the extent of caregiver involvement in child education for different living arrangements in 2010 and 2014. For children aged three to five, parents of urban intact families were significantly more involved than rural intact parents or caregivers of left-behind children, be it reading with the child or buying books for the child. Left-behind children with both parents away were especially deprived of caregiver involvement. Although caregiver involvement increased significantly from 2010 to 2014 for both rural intact children and left-behind children with both parents away, the gap in caregiver involvement remained considerable for children in different living arrangements.

For children aged 10 to 15, the advantage that children of urban intact families enjoyed in parental supervision and tutoring with homework over rural intact family and left-behind children in 2010 had almost disappeared in 2014. This was largely because of the large increase in the percentages of rural parents and caregivers of left-behind children who became involved. However, left-behind children with both parents away still tended to receive less caregiver support with homework tutoring compared to urban or rural intact families in 2014. A puzzling finding is that migrant children had much higher percentage of parental support with their schoolwork in 2010 than in 2014 and the drop in the percentage of homework supervision was a dramatic 20.7 percent. As migrant children were mostly urban dwellers, the decline in parental supervision was most likely a reflection of changing circumstances in their lives. Major cities such as Beijing have in recent years not only become much costlier to live in but have also instituted policies to make it more difficult for migrant children to get into school, thus keeping more of the migrant families separate.

Positive parenting behavior

Studies have found that, besides caregivers' involvement in children's educational activities, positive parenting behaviors, such as caregivers' encouragement on and reinforcement of children's positive behaviors and affectionate interaction between caregivers and children, can have a major impact on children's social, psychological, and cognitive development (Dornbusch et al. 1987; Li and Xie 2017). Positive parenting has also been shown to moderate the potentially adverse effect of poverty and material deprivation on the children's emotional and psychological development (Kiernan and Mensah 2011).

The CFPS includes a 12-item module on positive parenting behaviors as reported by children aged 10–15 in 2010 and 2014.[3] Through Varimax factor analysis, we identify three distinct factors representing different aspects of parenting behavior, which we term "encouragement," "engagement," and "interaction," and present the

Table 7.6.1 Positive parenting factor scores by community type (ages 10–15), 2014

Parenting behavior	Rural		Urban	
	Mean	S.E.	Mean	S.E.
Encouragement*	−0.053	0.046	0.114	0.065
Engagement*	−0.047	0.038	0.095	0.055
Interaction*	−0.078	0.035	0.223	0.062

Note: Sample size $N=1,448$, results are weighted. Analysis based on factor scores from a Varimax factor analysis of 12 items. * $p < 0.05$ level based on design-based Pearson chi-square statistic.

Table 7.6.2 Positive parenting factor scores by living arrangement (ages 10–15), 2014

Living Arrangement	Encouragement		Engagement		Interaction	
	Mean	Sig.	Mean	Sig.	Mean	Sig.
Rural intact	−0.061	a	0.019	ab	−0.049	ab
Urban intact	0.177	abc	0.077	cd	0.269	acde
LBC-no parent	−0.078	b	−0.238	ace	−0.108	c
LBC-1 parent	−0.009		−0.062		0.043	df
Migrant	0.129		0.193	e	0.067	g
Single-parent/orphan	−0.124	c	−0.178	bd	−0.260	befg

Note: Sample includes 10- to 15-year-old children, $N=1,448$.
The categories with the same superscripted letters are significantly different at $p < 0.05$ level.

results in Table 7.6 (for 2014 only; the 2010 numbers are broadly similar).[4] Our findings show that in 2014, as in 2010, the caregivers of children in rural areas ranked poorly in all three aspects of parenting behavior. When we disaggregate our findings by types of living arrangements (Table 7.6.2), we find that the caregivers of urban intact families were more likely to engage in positive parenting practices, especially concerning "encouragement" and "interaction," than caregivers in rural intact families and of left-behind children. Left-behind children with no parent at home suffered the most from lack of parental engagement but children with single parents or who are orphaned were the most vulnerable with respect to parents' interaction with them or lack thereof.

Attitudes on parental responsibility

Parents' attitudes on their responsibilities for raising children are important indicators of commitment to the healthy upbringing of their children. All too often, the issue of parental responsibility for children is entangled with considerations of marriage and especially of divorce. Studies in the US and other developed countries have pointed to the adverse effect of marriage dissolution, especially low-stress marriages, on child well-being (Booth and Amato 2001). Divorce often leads to major declines in social and economic resources and the displacement of the father from the family, which are shown to be detrimental to all aspects of child life (McLanahan, Tach, and Schneider 2013). In China, due to the pervasive social stigma associated with divorce and the lack of public assistance for single-parent families, the adverse effect of marriage dissolution on children can be especially acute (Dong, Wang, and Ollendick 2002; Liu et al. 2000).

The CFPS asked caregivers whether they agreed with four statements about parental responsibilities. These statements are: "Divorce is always harmful for children," "Even an unhappy marriage should be maintained for the sake of the child," "Parents should sacrifice their own welfare to save for their children's education," "I should take great responsibility for the child's grades at school." We summarize the caregivers' responses in Figure 7.1 and it is clear that the overwhelming majority of Chinese parents in both urban and rural areas agreed that parents were responsible for financing children's upbringing and education and, only slightly less so, for the children's academic performance at school. All too often, Chinese parents would do all they could, including making significant personal sacrifices, in order to save for and advance their children's education (Leung and Shek 2011). When we examined the responses by type of family living arrangement, we found no significant differences between caregivers of left-behind children and parents in intact families.

On the issue of divorce, the caregivers' responses are particularly noteworthy. As is well known, China has undergone enormous social upheaval through war, revolution, and reform. Whereas divorcees faced social opprobrium at the end of the Mao era, divorce is becoming commonplace today (Wang and Zhou 2010; Zhang, Wang, and Zhang 2014). Sometimes couples split up in order to bypass regulatory restrictions on property purchases and other matters.

The CFPS data are suggestive of the enormous tensions many parents feel about marriage, divorce, and the well-being of their children. 93 percent of urban parents and 84 percent of rural agreed that divorce

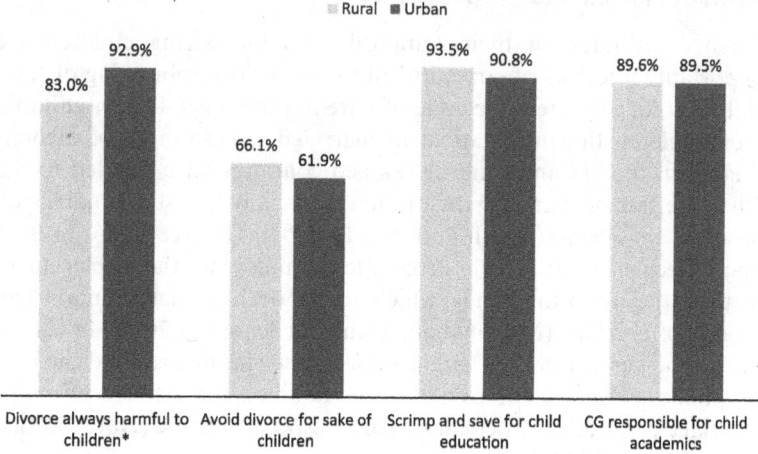

Figure 7.1 Attitudes on parental responsibility in rural and urban China, 2014
Note: Sample Size N = 3,716 in 2014. * p <.05 based on design-based Pearson chi-square statistic.

would be harmful to children. 62 and 66 percent of them respectively would avoid divorce and thus remain in an unhappy marriage for the sake of the child. The differences of 30 percent urban and 18 percent rural mean that these respondents would seek a divorce even though they recognized the harm divorce would inflict on children. It is noteworthy that urban parents were significantly more likely to agree that divorce is harmful to children than rural parents but were also more willing to divorce.

We also disaggregated these responses by types of living arrangement (Table not shown for the sake of space). The parents with left-behind children were less cognizant that divorce would be harmful to children. However, a remarkably high 74 percent of the caregivers of left-behind children by both parents (LBC-no parent) chose "avoid divorce for the sake of the child." In contrast, only 60 percent of parents who were split, with one parent staying at home with their child/children (LBC-1 parent), agreed with the same statement.

Summary and discussion

In this chapter, we have examined the community and family contexts for China's children in 2010 and 2014. While urban-rural disparities attract our attention, the improvements rural communities experienced during that period also stand out. Meanwhile, the family environments of children in rural areas greatly improved. More rural children enjoyed a stimulating home environment conducive to learning and more caregivers were buying books and reading stories to their children. Chinese parents, both urban and rural, showed heightened awareness of the importance of parental involvement in their children's upbringing and were willing to make substantial personal sacrifices to help their offspring in education and beyond.

Progress aside, consistent urban-rural disparities still exist in multiple aspects of family context such as home environment, parenting behavior, and support for school work. Left-behind children with no parent at home were especially vulnerable.

Considering the long-term effects of healthy early childhood development for improving adult outcomes (Heckman, Pinto, and Savelyev 2013), it is imperative that the Chinese government's efforts at poverty alleviation should go beyond mere provision of income benefits and nutrition assistance for poor families. Besides investing in quality child care centers, kindergartens, and early childhood education facilities in rural areas, child welfare administrators may consider the adoption of intervention measures to imbibe rural caregivers with knowledge of child development and teach them appropriate parenting practices that are found wanting (Luo et al. 2017; Yue et al. 2017). The Chinese government may also consider scaling up the home visiting models that have been proved effective in China and abroad (China Development Research Foundation 2017).

Notes

1 The questions included in CFPS 2010 were different from the 2014 wave on respondents' relations with neighbors and relatives but the patterns of the responses are similar. For the sake of space and clarity, we have omitted the table using 2010 data.
2 For "read to child," reading to child at least once a month as reported by caregiver is required to meet the criteria. "Buy books" means buy children's books at least several times a year, also reported by caregiver. "Homework supervision" means caregiver demanding child complete homework at least twice a week. "Tutoring" means caregiver checking on child's homework at least twice a week. Both are reported by caregivers.
3 Parenting style refers to the three factors extracted through factor analysis of child-reported frequencies of 12 parenting behaviors: (1) encouragement: the caregiver encourages the child in study and independent problem-solving, uses fair rules and reasoning in handling problematic behaviors;

(2) engagement: caregivers help with homework and learn about school activities; and (3) interaction: caregivers talk and play with children, and tell stories.
4 The descriptive statistics for the three factor scores are: encourage (M=0, SD=.84), engage (M=0, SD=.83), interact (M=0, SD=.74).

8 Youth values and attitudes

Having safe, healthy and well-educated children is vital to the future of a society and the sustainable development of our planet. Hence we have so far focused on various aspects of the well-being of China's children and youth and noted the progress that has been made and the challenges that remain.

Yet children and youth are not only charges to be taken care of but also stakeholders of the present and makers of the future. Not leaving matters to chance, the Chinese Communist Party has the Communist Youth League to inculcate and incorporate the younger generations into the communist establishment. Successive Chinese leaders have also appealed to youth. Mao famously likened youth to the morning sun and held out that the world would ultimately be theirs. In his keynote speech to the 19th Party Congress held in 2017, Chinese Communist Party General Secretary Xi Jinping spoke directly "to all our young people, you should have firm ideals and convictions, aim high, and have your feet firmly on the ground (Xi 2017)."

To better understand the present and gain insight into the future of a society, we should also try our best to know the younger generation in its various formations. In particular, youth attitudes toward social and political issues, when contrasted with those of the older generations, may open windows to future social and cultural shifts and allow us to gain insight into China's political development.

The literature on Chinese youth values and attitudes has offered divergent perspectives on China's youth. On the one hand, some scholars propose that China's post-Mao Reform and Open Door policies have not only provided room for market forces but also space for individualism, autonomy, and the waning of the traditional family hierarchy (Naftali 2009; Jankowiak and Moore 2017). As a result, the post-1980s and post-1990s cohorts, who have grown up during China's economic boom, are likely to be less deferential to authoritarian leadership (Li 2015). On the other hand, other studies have pointed to the strong sentiments of nationalism among a generation that has been exposed to sustained patriotic education and suggest that these youths may not be as open as thought (Tang and Darr 2012; Zhao 2013; Zhao 2014). There is also the possibility that, for the generation that has grown up amid rising prosperity, their attitudes may be more contingent on the trajectory of China's future economic and political development (Fish 2015).

To help frame our investigation of the attitudes and values of Chinese youths based on data from the CFPS surveys, we draw on the "modernization theory," which has regained much prominence in studies based on the World Value Survey (Inglehart 1971; Inglehart and Welzel 2005; Dalton and Welzel 2014). In a nutshell, modernization theory argues that as modernization occurs people will become less religious, less submissive to authority, more supportive to gender equality, and demand more political participation (Inglehart 2007). Therefore, to provide a comparable overview of Chinese youth's attitudes and values, we utilize the CFPS data to delve into four topics—deference to authority, gender equality, social inequality, and political satisfaction. In contrast to earlier chapters, this chapter centers on youth between the ages of 16 and 24.

Consistent with popular Chinese perceptions and the relevant literature, we analyze the CFPS data by birth-year cohorts (Fish 2015; Li 2015). For example, the "1990s birth cohort" represents those born between 1990 to 1999, and is commonly referred to as the "post-90s" in China (Fish 2015). Such categorization allows us to trace the change of values within each cohort as they age, and thereby to conduct cohort analysis to understand how Chinese cohorts differ in values and attitudes (Inglehart 2007).

Deference to authority

In studies of political values, deference to authority (in family, workplace, and in politics) is a reliable and important measure of political culture (Dalton and Welzel 2014). In comparative terms, higher deference to authority is characteristic of a more "traditional" society that prioritizes social order over individual autonomy.

In Lucian Pye's (1992) incisive probe into Chinese political culture, familial hierarchy in the Chinese society was the psychological foundation for people's acquiescence toward and consent to despotic authority. Since Chinese society has gone through enormous economic changes in the direction of the market, we expect to find significant value changes among different cohort groups. More specifically, we expect the younger cohorts, who have grown up in materially far more prosperous times, to be more individualistic than the older cohorts (and generations). Various media reports suggest that the younger cohorts, empowered by freer access to information and social connections, seek greater freedom in their private life (Yang 2018).

In the CFPS survey, there are two questions probing the respondents' conformity to authority and both relate to authority in families. Since the Chinese phrase for state or country, *guojia* 国家, is in fact a combination of *guo* (country) and *jia* (family), it is not a stretch to suggest that our findings about authority relations within the family can also be used to illuminate attitudes toward the country/state.

The two CFPS questions ask whether children should "give up their own will and submit to their parents' wish," and whether one of the respondent's main goals in life is "to make parents proud." Overall, youth in the CFPS survey differed markedly in their answers to the two questions. As shown in Figure 8.1, while 76.3 percent of the post-90s

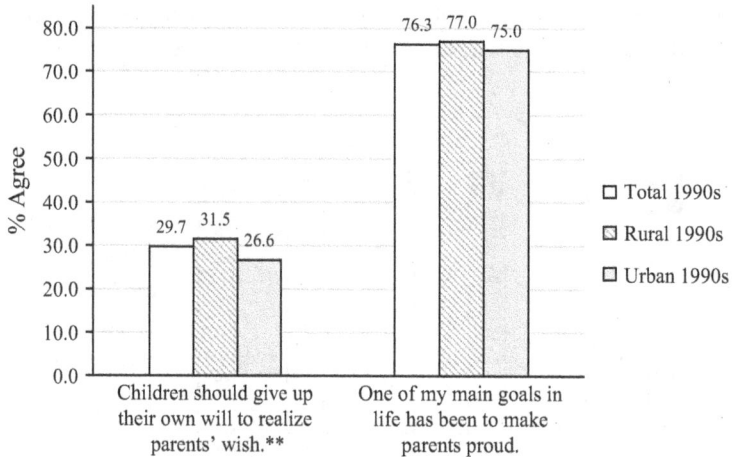

Figure 8.1 Deference to parental authority among the 1990s cohort

Note: Weighted Percentage. Sample size $N = 3,391$ for "realize parents' wish"; $N = 2,329$ for "make parents proud." ** $p < 0.01$ for percentages based on design-based Pearson chi-square statistic. The "90s cohort" is defined as those respondents born between 1990 to 1999.

Source: CFPS (2014 and 2010).

80 Youth values and attitudes

cohort agreed that one of their main goals in life was to make their parents proud, less than 30 percent of them answered that they should give up their own will to realize their parents' wishes.

How should we interpret this set of answers? We submit that the remarkable difference between the answers to the two questions may suggest the younger Chinese generation's sharply reduced deference to parental authority. While they wanted to make parents "proud," they were, contrary to traditional Confucian precepts of hierarchical parent-child relationships, far less willing to satisfy their parents by sacrificing their own will. When analyzed separately, rural and urban youth in the 1990s cohort were agreed on the question of making parents proud. On the question of sacrificing one's own will, however, the urban respondents were even less willing than the rural respondents.

Data from CFPS 2014 allows us to conduct a cohort comparison on the first question. As shown in Figure 8.2, the post-90s cohort showed the least agreement with the statement that children should be subjected to their parents' will. In contrast, the older the respondents, the more they showed deference to parental authority. The urban-rural differences in answers to this question are also worth revisiting. Within the 1990s cohort, nearly 42 percent of urban youth disagreed with the idea of sacrificing their own will, compared with only 30 percent of the rural 1990s cohort (Figure omitted for the sake of space).

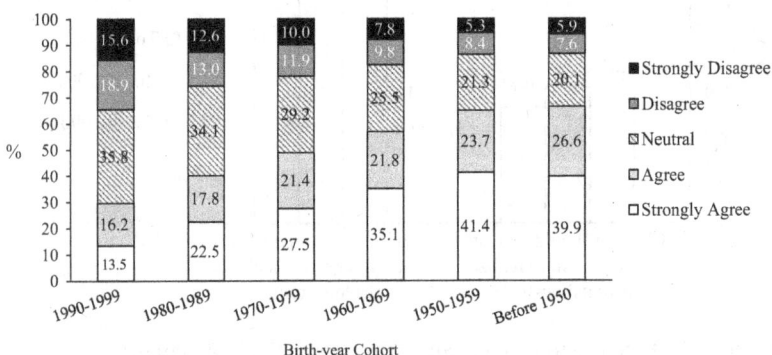

Figure 8.2 "Children should give up their own will to realize parents' wishes"**
Note: Weighted Percentage. Sample size $N = 29,408$. ** $p < 0.01$ for percentages based on design-based Pearson chi-square statistic.
Source: CFPS (2014).

Gender roles and patrilineality

In the CFPS questionnaire, three questions on marriage, family, and having children relate directly to the issue of gender roles and expectations (see Figure 8.3 legend). The respondents' answers show clearly that the younger generation in China is much less willing to adhere to traditional expectations about gender roles and patrilineal values.

As Figure 8.3 shows, the older the cohort, the more the respondents agreed with the traditional gender role statements. More than 80 percent of the respondents born before 1950 agreed that a woman needed children to be fulfilled, less than half of the 1990s cohort thought the same. This trend also applies to the other two statements. The 1990s cohort showed the least agreement with these statements. Overall, the CFPS data reveal powerful generational differences in attitudes toward gender roles in Chinese society.

One question in the CFPS questionnaire—"One needs to have at least one son to carry on the family lineage"—was included to probe respondents' attitudes toward patrilineality, the idea that only sons have the right, as well as the obligation, to inherit family lineage. This

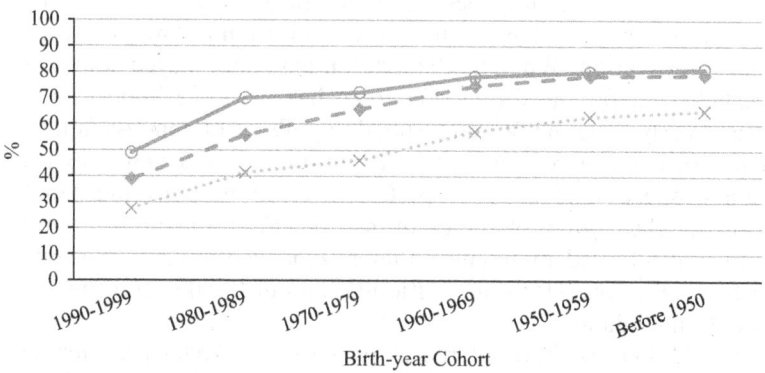

Figure 8.3 Woman's gender role, by cohort
Note: Weighted percentage. Sample size $N = 29{,}512$. * $p < 0.05$ for percentages based on design-based Pearson chi-square statistic.
Source: CFPS (2014).

82 Youth values and attitudes

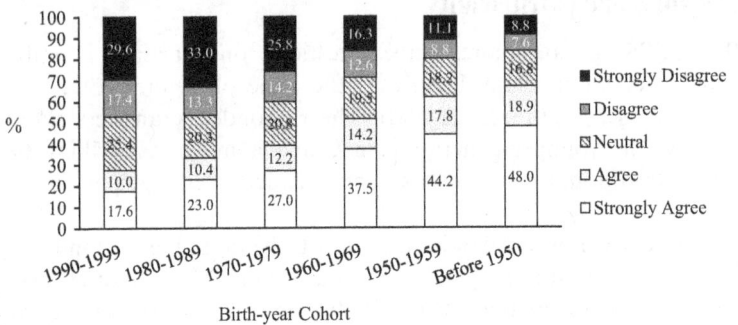

Figure 8.4 "One needs to have at least one son to carry on the family lineage"
Note: Weighted percentage. Sample size N = 31,506.
Source: CFPS (2014).

is distinctively a patriarchy norm that associates the male gender with authority in the family and lineage (Hu and Scott 2014; Jankowiak and Moore 2017; Xie 2013). The CFPS survey (Figure 8.4) reveals that nearly 67 percent of the respondents born before 1950 (age 65 or older) agreed with the "needs son" statement whereas less than 28 percent of the 1990s cohort were in agreement. Indeed, fully 47 percent of the 1990s cohort and 46 percent of the 1980s cohort either disagreed or strongly disagreed with the statement.

The extent to which these generational differences in attitudes toward patrilineal values is due to modernization is a matter for further investigation. While modernization may have played some role, we believe a far more powerful force has been the imposition of strict family planning, which resulted in millions of son-less families. The growing disagreement with the "needs son" statement may thus be a strong case of adaptive preference as more and more people, realizing the high probability of not having a son in the family, increased adopted preferences that rationalized actually permitted fertility practices. This is a question that awaits further scrutiny with longitudinal data.

In addition to cohort differences, the CFPS 2014 data also show significant variations between rural and urban, as well as between male and female respondents. Among the 1990s cohort (Figure 8.5) for instance, male respondents are substantially more likely to agree with traditional gender roles than female respondents and the same pattern exists for rural vs. urban respondents.

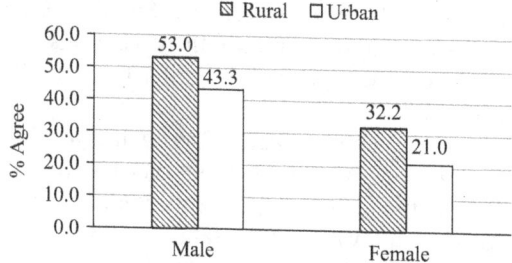

Figure 8.5 Men should prioritize career; women should prioritize family, the 1990s cohort

Note: Weighted percentage. Sample size N = 3,392 (rural = 2,456; urban = 936).
Source: CFPS (2014).

Scholars studying gender dynamics and household division of labor in China maintain that Chinese women are increasingly enabled to assert their interest in family life, as gender equality was not only emphasized in Maoist China but also further accentuated by the strict family planning policies of the post-Mao era (Jankowiak and Moore 2017). Chinese women's labor force participation rate, at 63 percent as of 2016, is higher than in most developed countries such as the US (55 percent) (World Bank 2017). Yet the revealed pattern of attitudes toward gender roles, based on CFPS 2014, suggests that even among the younger cohorts of respondents, there remain persistent gaps in attitudes toward gender roles between Chinese men and women, and between rural and urban residents.

Attitudes toward and perceptions of social inequality and mobility

Besides attitudes toward authority relations and gender equality, another important indicator for taking a measure of a society is how open it is to talent and how easy it is for the talented to move up the ladder of success. In making his argument that it was but a myth to characterize Chinese society of the 2000s as a "social volcano", Whyte (2010a; 2010b) reported that the Chinese public at the time saw plenty of opportunity for upward mobility and were quite accepting of the rising inequality that had become quite large by then. Such public attitudes could be interpreted as conducive to social and political stability. Since youth impelled by a strong sense of societal unfairness and injustice

84 Youth values and attitudes

can potentially be especially disruptive of the status quo, whether during the Tiananmen Crisis of 1989 or elsewhere (e.g. Sun 1991), it is highly appropriate we focus on children and youth perceptions of social inequality in China and how these perceptions differ from those of adults of different age cohorts.

In the baseline CFPS 2010 survey, children aged 12 to 14 and youths and adults older than 16 were asked to give their opinions on what would make a child successful.[1] Among the factors respondents could choose from were hard work, (naturally endowed) talent, family connections (*guanxi*), family social status, and family wealth. Figure 8.6 plots the responses by age for respondents who were 30 years old or younger (12–14; 16–30).

As Figure 8.6 shows, close to 90 percent of Chinese children and youth between 12 and 30 believed hard work was the route for a child to become successful, double the percentage of those who chose (naturally endowed) talent as the source of success. This is an incredibly important measure of youthful optimism that they can get ahead by working hard. It is consistent with Whyte (2010a), who found that the Chinese general public believed that one's education level, which itself is a function of hard work, and the ability to work hard contributed most to one's success.

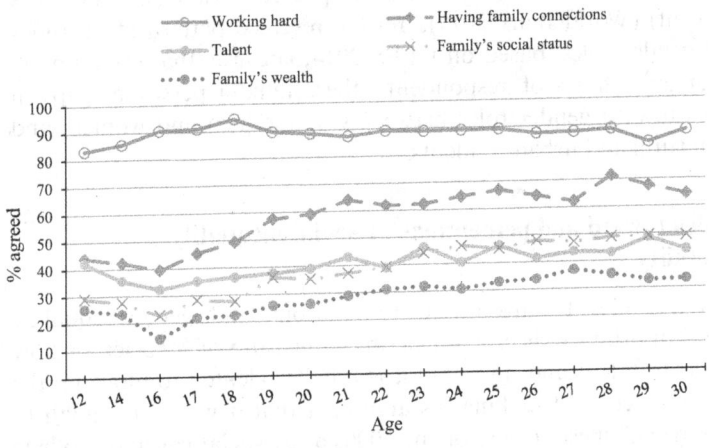

Figure 8.6 "What would make a child successful in the future?", age 12 to 30

Note: Sample size $N = 8,135$. Percentage presented are sum of "strongly agree" and "agree" for each condition as important for one to become successful, as asked in the CFPS survey. Results are weighted.

Source: CFPS (2010).

Yet China is also well known for being the land of *guanxi*, or personal relationships and connections (Yang 1994). Thus it is not a surprise that "having family connections" was ranked second on the list of reasons for a child to achieve success in the future. This was particularly the case for youth aged 19 and above, who would have increasingly had to think about or to find employment and other opportunities (cf. Hanser 2002). Having (naturally endowed) talent or social status were ranked further below. Strikingly, having family wealth came in last as a factor influencing a child's future success.

In Table 8.1, we compare responses to the same question across decadal cohorts. We also group the list of possible factors influencing a child's future achievement into three groups: family resources; uncontrollable factors (natural talent and luck); and self-determined factors including hard work and education. We recognize these are rough categories and some of the factors may not fit perfectly into the categories. Natural talent and even luck may not be random and

Table 8.1 What would make a child successful in the future (%), by cohort

Success factors/cohort		1990–1999	1980–1989	1970–1979	1960–1969	1950–1959	Before 1950
Family resources	Average	**33.72**	**47.53**	**49.08**	**53.41**	**56.68**	**51.71**
	Family's social status**	29.74	45.11	48.22	51.50	54.95	50.99
	Family's wealth**	22.67	32.58	36.15	42.18	48.40	45.90
	Family's connections**	48.76	64.89	62.87	66.56	66.70	58.25
Uncontrollable factors	Average	**36.38**	**47.00**	**46.06**	**52.45**	**54.56**	**48.27**
	(Naturally endowed) talent**	36.88	43.61	45.57	51.93	52.90	48.17
	Luck**	35.87	50.39	46.55	52.96	56.22	48.37
Self-determined factors	Average	**81.60**	**81.55**	**82.25**	**83.69**	**80.11**	**75.03**
	Working hard**	89.23	88.00	85.76	86.46	81.16	75.96
	Education level**	73.96	75.10	78.74	80.91	79.05	74.10

Note: Results weighted. Sample size $N = 34,719$. Percentages presented are sum of "strongly agree" and "agree" for each condition as important for one to become successful, as asked in the CFPS survey. Results weighted. † $p <0.1$, * $p <0.05$, ** $p <0.01$ based on design-based Pearson chi-square statistic.

Source: CFPS (2010).

can often be influenced by family circumstances and community endowments. A person's education owes a lot to grit and hard work but a person's educational achievement is also often influenced by family resources.

With these caveats in mind, we note that the cohorts after 1960—those that came of age in the post-Mao era and have been able to take advantage of China's reform policies—ranked hard work especially highly even though the 1950s cohort and the pre-1950 group also thought hard work was the most influential factor for success.

On the factor of family resources, it is worth noting that with the 1950s cohort and after, the younger the cohort, the less members of that cohort considered family resources to be important in influencing a child's success. Here the variations are quite interesting in that family connections were considered to be more important than family social status and family wealth. Note especially that the 1980s and 1990s cohorts had low regard for the importance of family wealth. Yet we should also keep in mind that family wealth may be translatable into connections and even social status.

Overall, except for the pre-1950s group, which went through many political upheavals in their lifetimes, members of the older cohorts tended to select more of the factors as having influence on a child's future achievement than the younger cohorts. In other words, hard work and education were considered by overwhelming majorities of each cohort as important—an indication that most of the Chinese population considered Chinese society as open to upward mobility, but as a respondent got older, he/she was more likely to also select the other factors—from connections to raw talent to luck—as being also influential. With age came wisdom.

Political satisfaction and dissatisfaction

The CFPS 2014 questionnaire included questions for gauging public assessment of the Chinese Party-state or government performance in ten domains or issue areas. Respondents were asked to rate each domain or issue area based on their perception of how serious the issue was. The ten issue areas were clean government, justice, health care, employment, rich-poor gap, social insurance, education, housing, public safety (社会治安), and environmental protection. In the cases of public safety (or social order) and justice (司法公正), respondents were asked to rate how good the public safety situation or the state of justice was.

Since this chapter focuses on the attitudes and values of youth, we present the summary evaluations offered by youth, divided into urban

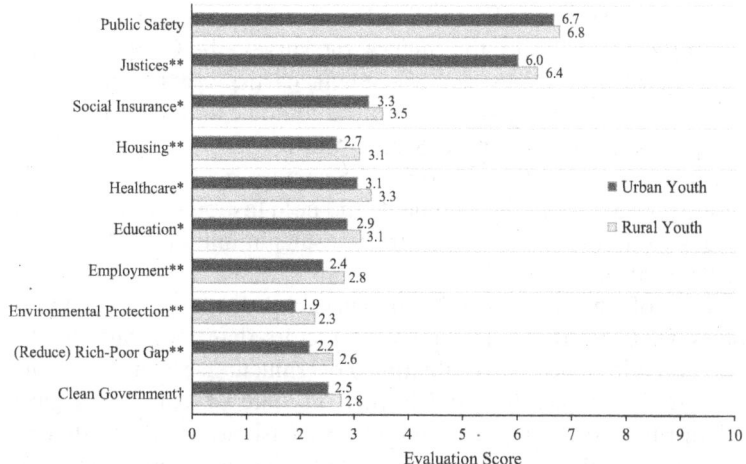

Figure 8.7 Evaluation of government performance by community type, 1990s cohort

Note: Sample size varies between 3,374 to 3,389 depending on the question. The given score range is from 0 to 10. Scores are recoded so that a higher score indicates a better evaluation. Youth is defined as those respondents born in or after 1990, who were aged from 16 to 24 at the time of survey. Results weighted. † p <0.1, * p <0.05, ** p <0.01 for post-estimation t-test of means between rural and urban youth.
Source: CFPS (2014).

and rural components for each measure, in Figure 8.7. We also compare the evaluations offered by youth with those of the general population.

As Figure 8.7. shows, Chinese youth between the ages of 16–24 essentially gave failing grades to the Chinese authorities on their performance in areas from corruption (clean government) to education and health care, and to housing and social insurance. These evaluations were, not surprisingly, lower than those given by the general population. The largest disagreement between youth and the general population was on environmental protection, with a 0.81 mean score difference. On public safety and justice, however, Chinese youth gave passing marks. We do want to note, however, that, because of how these questions were phrased and framed, the responses to all ten items may not be strictly comparable.

On all the issues except public safety, urban youth were more dissatisfied with government performance than rural youth. This was especially the case with environmental protection or pollution, inequality (rich-poor gap), employment, and housing. Since the scores given by both urban and rural youth as well as the general population were quite low, it appears that, as of the time of the survey, the Chinese leadership was faced with deep social discontent, particularly among youth. Given a political opening, such discontent could be mobilized to pose a challenge to the powers that be. Seen in this context, the strong efforts by the newly ascendant CCP General Secretary Xi Jinping to tackle corruption, clean up the environment, and hold fast on stability seemed to have been designed with such survey results in mind (MacFarquhar 2015; Yang 2017a; Yang 2017b).

In view of the urban-rural differences we discussed in previous chapters, we can advance a number of factors that contribute to the urban-rural differences in evaluating government performance. One hypothesis that comes to mind is that, in spite of continuing gaps in urban-rural well-being on multiple dimensions, rural youth had experienced significantly more rapid improvement well-being than urban youth. The narrowing in the urban-rural well-being gap may have thus helped rural youth to be more satisfied than urban youth, who have had to increasingly contend with various quality of life issues (Wu, Yang, and Chen 2017). An alternative hypothesis is that the urban-rural gap in satisfaction with government performance may be at least partly due to an information gap. According to a CNNIC report released in August 2017, only 26.7 percent of the total Chinese internet users are rural residents (CNNIC 2017). Because they were less exposed to negative information, rural youth tended to be somewhat more positive about government performance than urban youth.

Summary and conclusion

Chinese political orthodoxy continues to harken to the familial hierarchy that Pye (1992) had considered to be central in understanding Chinese political psychology. In seeking to inculcate patriotism among youth, Chinese authorities typically mix love of country with love of the CCP (Nie 2008).

Having grown up during an era of unprecedented growth and prosperity, the younger cohorts of China, products of the family planning regime, are carriers of a generational shift in values and attitudes. Based on the CFPS data, it is interesting to note that Chinese youth tend to be less deferential to traditional authority, less supportive of patrilineal values, and more confident that one can get ahead by working hard. As they have become more independent, their expectations about government performance also appear to have risen and thus they have become quite critical of government performance in many areas.

The CFPS data thus reveal a substantial generational shift in political attitudes and values among Chinese youth and a nascent turn in the direction of post-materialism and self-expressiveness Inglehart (2009) and Dalton and Welzel (2014). Such a turn could be fundamentally at variance with the Chinese leadership's strong top-down approach. There is anecdotal evidence that China's millennials are already leading a quiet revolution in some respects (Yang 2018).

Note

1 We utilize data from CFPS 2010 here for comparison across age cohorts because the same set of questions was asked only for respondents aged 16 to 21 in CFPS 2014.

9 Migration and parental absence for left-behind children

In laying out the institutional and policy context for our study in Chapter 2, we highlighted how massive migration has gone hand in hand with China's rapid industrialization and urbanization in the last three decades. On a scale that dwarfed the great migrations that occurred in the era of industrialization in developed economies (e.g. Handlin 2002), the Chinese version of the Great Migration has seen tens of millions of rural residents in China trek to urban areas in the coastal region to escape from subsistence farming and seek better job opportunities in manufacturing and service sectors.

While moving within their own country, most Chinese migrant workers have found it exceedingly difficult to settle down permanently in the host or destination cities because of structural inequalities, especially the household registration system, and exclusionary policies adopted by large metropolitan areas. In consequence, children of migrant workers are often barred from access to the urban public education system (Yiu and Yun 2017). Migrants must also contend with low-end jobs, job insecurity, poor housing conditions, and high living costs in urban areas. As a result, migrants from rural areas who are parents with children often make the difficult decision of leaving their children behind in the care of the mother only or of the grandparents if both parents migrate to other areas to work. The issue of left-behind children is one of the most salient features of Chinese-style development.

The plight of left-behind children has attracted much attention and sympathy in recent years. Some of the left-behind children, lacking proper supervision and care from parents, have been vulnerable to injuries, sickness, and acts of violence. Several incidents involving the death of left-behind children, such as the death of four siblings in poverty stricken Bijie, Guizhou in 2015, have provoked great public concern and strong demands for the establishment of a child protection system in China (Xinhua Net 2015).

Given the massive scale of the internal migration in China and the number of children affected by it, we revisit and zero in on the issue of left-behind children in this and the next chapters. In this chapter we draw on the CFPS data to look in greater detail at the extent and patterns of parental migration and their impact on the family structure and living arrangements of children. We also discuss the potential adverse effects of extended parental absence on the short- and long-term development of children. In the next chapter, we present more analysis with a focus on child development outcomes.

Urbanization, exclusion, and migration patterns

We begin with a summary of Chinese children's living situations based on data from the CFPS baseline survey of 2010. As Table 9.1 shows, more than 30 percent of children in rural areas experienced parental absence (either parent or both), while about 20 percent of urban children were in the same situation.[1] The primary reason for parental absence in China is not due to parental divorce, desertion, or death—factors which combined affected less than 5 percent of all children—but because of parents migrating away from home in pursuit of job opportunities that tend to be concentrated in certain regions.

There are two definitions of left-behind children. The broad definition, as given by UNICEF (2014), includes all children with at least one parent away as left-behind children. Seeking to delimit the issue, the relevant authorities in China have increasingly adopted a narrow definition of left-behind children as those with both parents absent from home in pursuit of job opportunities (NBS et al. 2017; State Council 2016b).

The CFPS data on Chinese children's living arrangements show that parental absence for left-behind children, following the broad definition, is almost a half-and-half split, with 47.3 percent of left-behind children having both parents away (the narrow definition) while 52.7 percent had one parent home and the other away. Among the latter group, most left-behind children had the father away and the mother home. This indicates the continuity of traditional gender roles and household division of labor, with mothers taking care of most housework and child rearing while fathers worked away from home as the breadwinner.

It is well known that the spatial patterns of internal migration are a function of China's regional development strategies (Yang 1996). The sources of migrant labor tend to be located in the less-developed central and western regions, especially in demographic powerhouses such as Henan and Sichuan Provinces, whereas provinces and cities such as

Table 9.1 Characteristics of children in different living situations in China

Variable	Living situation: parents present or absent (%)				
	Both parents absent	Father absent	Mother absent	Both parents present	Total
All children	13.1	11.6	3.2	72.1	100
Community type *					
Rural	15.0	12.2	3.3	69.5	100
Urban	7.9	10.1	2.7	79.4	100
Age *					
0 to 5	15.1	13.2	2.5	69.2	100
6 to 10	14.1	10.2	3.5	72.2	100
11 to 15	9.9	11.2	3.6	75.3	100
Gender					
Female	13.3	12.4	2.8	71.5	100
Male	12.9	11.0	3.5	72.7	100
Ethnicity *					
Ethnic minority	13.6	9.3	2.4	74.7	100
Han	13.0	12.1	3.3	71.6	100
Hukou registration *					
Rural	14.6	12.1	3.3	70.0	100
Urban	8.3	10.0	2.8	79.0	100
Region *					
Eastern (coastal)	7.8	12.1	3.2	76.9	100
Central	16.4	11.6	3.4	68.6	100
Western	15.8	11.1	2.8	70.3	100
Living arrangement *					
Rural intact family				100.0	100
Urban intact family				100.0	100
Left-behind children (broad definition)	47.3	44.9	7.8		100 100
Migrant children	14.0	9.2	1.4	75.4	100
Single-parent/orphan	42.1	27.8	30.1		100

Note: 2010 CFPS child sample N=8,990. Numbers shown are weighted percentages.
* p <.05 based on designed-based Pearson chi-square statistic.

Guangdong, Beijing and Shanghai are major destinations for migrants (Cai 1999; Fan 1999). Residents in the eastern region, in contrast, can find job opportunities locally or near their home and are less likely to migrate or migrate long distances far away from home.

Table 9.2 Local or inter-provincial migration patterns of parents of left-behind children

Home region	Father's work place (%)			Mother's work place (%)		
	Other province	Home province	Total	Other province	Home province	Total
Eastern	37	63	100	36	64	100
Central	64	36	100	87	13	100
Western	68	32	100	91	9	100
Total	57	43	100	78	22	100

Note: 2010 CFPS child sample $N=1,484$. Numbers shown are weighted percentages.

The regional patterns of parental absence clearly mirror the patterns of migration. In the more developed eastern region, where many of the destination cities are located, 77 percent of the children had parents at home, about 7 percentage points higher than in the central and western regions. In other words, parents, including mothers, in the western and central regions are more likely to migrate and leave their children behind than in the east (see Table 9.2). The numbers are especially striking: 8 percent of children in the eastern region had no parents at home, compared with about 16 percent of children in the western and central regions (see Table 9.1).

Tables 9.2 and 9.3 offer a statistical birds-eye view of the inter-provincial and inter-regional migration patterns of the parents of left-behind children (broad definition). Table 9.2 indicates that most parents of left-behind children in the western and central regions worked outside of their home province, while most parents in the eastern region found jobs within their home province.

Table 9.3 shows the cross-region migration patterns of parents in the three regions. A vast majority of migrant parents in the eastern region stayed in the eastern region, while most parents of left-behind children in the central and west regions travelled to the eastern region to find jobs. There were some differences in the inter-regional migratory patterns of fathers and mothers that appear to be a function of job availability. As seen in Table 9.3, migrant mothers in all three regions were more likely than fathers to work in the eastern region. While migrant mothers in the eastern region remained in the eastern region, 10 percent of the fathers in the eastern region worked in other regions. In the western and central regions, about 80 percent of the migratory mothers headed to the eastern region, while less than 70 percent of the migratory fathers did.

Table 9.3 Inter-regional migration patterns of parents of left-behind children

Home region	Father's work region (%)			
	Eastern	Central	Western	Total
Eastern	90	8	2	100
Central	69	27	5	100
Western	64	6	30	100
Total	73	15	12	100

Home region	Mother's work region (%)			
	Eastern	Central	Western	Total
Eastern	97	1	2	100
Central	81	16	3	100
Western	79	5	16	100
Total	84	9	8	100

Note: 2010 CFPS child sample *N*=1,484. Numbers shown are weighted percentages.

While all left-behind children experienced extended parental absence, those in the central and western region suffered the most, as the long travel distance and higher transportation cost made it more difficult for their parents to visit home regularly (Liu and Erwin 2015). For most migrant parents working on the eastern coast, the annual long journey home during the Chinese New Year was an ordeal (The Economist 2015; Phillips 2015).

Experiences of parental absence for left-behind children

The early childhood years are critical for healthy development of children's physical, psychological and cognitive capabilities (Phillips and Shonkoff 2000). Parental absence in the earlier years of childhood can thus be especially detrimental to a child's well-being (Liu, Li, and Ge 2009). In this section, we rely on the CFPS data to offer more details of children's experiences with parental absence, including the age distribution of children who are left behind and the timing and duration of parental absence.

Figure 9.1 shows the rate of parental absence for all children from newborn to age 15. Nearly 30 percent of all one year olds experienced parental absence of one or both parents. For two year olds, the rate of parental absence rose to 35 percent, including 20 percent with neither parent at home. The prevalence of parental absence peaked at 37 percent (one or no parent at home) with four year olds. For rural areas only,

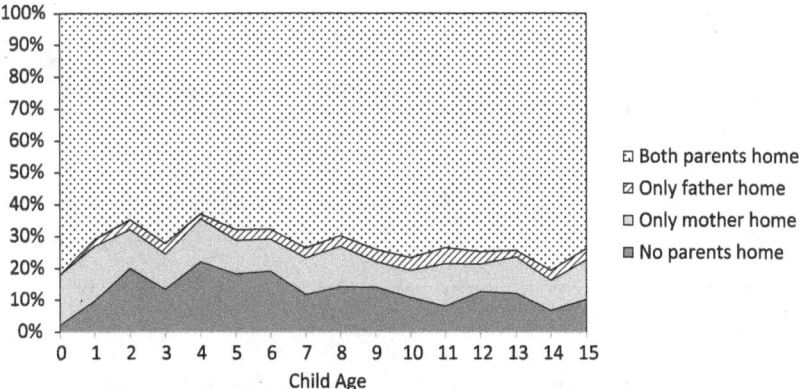

Figure 9.1 Child living arrangements by child age in 2010

more than 40 percent of the four-year-old children had one (15 percent) or both parents (25 percent) absent.

The prevalence of parental absence declined somewhat with older children, but was still at 20 percent for children of 14 years old. As expected, a regional break-down shows that, for each age group, a higher percentage of children in the western and central regions experienced parental absence than children in the eastern region. More than a quarter of children of younger age groups had no parent at home in the western region and thus spent their early childhood years with little parental care or supervision.

CFPS 2014 data allow us to calculate the duration of parental absence/presence in 2014. Figures 9.2 and 9.3 show the percentages of children at each age who lived with their father or mother for a certain number of months during the year. The proportion of children whose fathers were at home for less than one month of the year was 10 percent at age one but increased to 17 percent at age four and would remain above 17 percent for later ages. If we include the 12 to 20 percent children whose fathers were at home for only two to four months in the previous year, the total percentage of children who experienced extended absence of their fathers were over 20 percent at age one and more than 30 percent at age four and later years.

The graph (Figure 9.3) for mother's presence is somewhat reassuring at the start. Most left-behind children broadly defined were in the care of their mothers. At age one, 7 percent of children had mothers who were away for extended periods. However, the percentage of mothers

96 Migration and parental absence

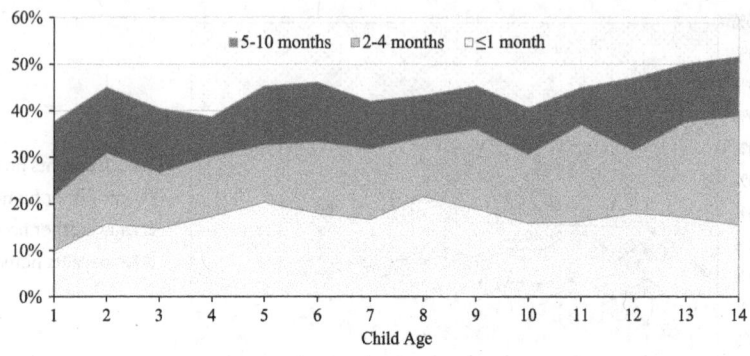

Figure 9.2 Months children had father at home in 2014 by child age

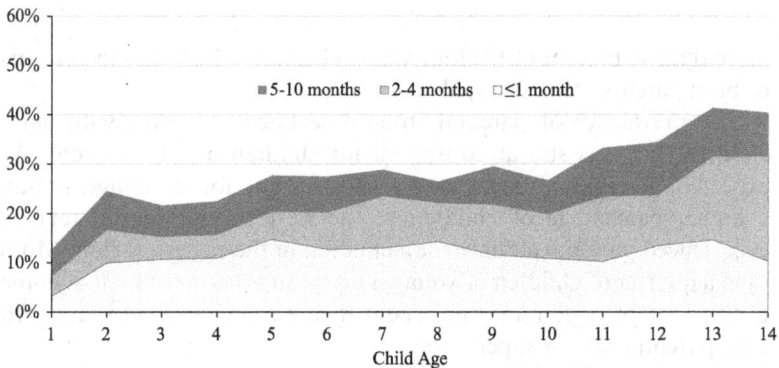

Figure 9.3 Months child had mother at home in 2014 by child age

who left their children behind for an extended period quickly increased to 15 percent at age two and 20 percent at age five. For teenage children, especially after they got to middle school, over 30 percent had mothers who were away for extended periods.

Separate analysis indicates that, as of 2014, about 20 percent of all children experienced extended parental absence of both father and mother; that is to say, they have had neither of their parents at home for most of the past year. As noted earlier, there were strong regional patterns. Children of the central and western regions (interior regions) were more likely to experience long periods of parental absence, especially that of mothers, than children of the eastern region (see Table 9.4).

Table 9.4 Months children had father or mother at home in 2014 by region (%)

Regions	Months father at home				
	<=1 month	2–4 months	5–10 months	>=11 months	Total
Eastern	15	15	11	59	100
Central	19	16	13	51	100
Western	17	16	14	53	100
Total	17	16	12	55	100
	Months mother at home				
	<=1 month	2–4 months	5–10 months	>=11 months	Total
Eastern	8	9	6	77	100
Central	15	10	8	67	100
Western	12	12	11	65	100
Total	11	10	8	71	100

Note: 2014 CFPS child sample $N=8,300$. Numbers shown are weighted percentages.

15 and 12 percent of children in the central and western regions respectively did not have their mothers at home for almost the whole year. The comparable number for children of the eastern region was 8 percent.

Patterns of care-giving for children, especially left-behind children

Past studies have shown the importance of parental care for child health and development, especially in early childhood (Amato 1991, 2005; Walker et al. 2011). Besides the health benefits of breastfeeding for children (Ip et al. 2007), the secure attachment and close relationship formed between the mother and infant child are the foundation for child psychological and emotional health. When such attachment or relationship is lacking, children's development can be severely compromised. For example, in the US, the number of skipped families, where children stay with grandparents due to their parents' incarceration, death, drug abuse, or child neglect, has been on the rise in recent decades (Hayslip and Kaminski 2005). Studies have found that these custodial grandchildren tend to have higher levels of emotional and behavioral difficulties and poorer academic performance than children in other family configurations (Dunifon 2013; Pittman 2007; Pittman and Boswell 2007; Smith and Palmieri 2007).

Whether we follow the broad or narrow definition of the term "left-behind children," the sheer number of left-behind children in China is enormous in global terms. Common sense and the existing literature thus call for a better understanding of the impact of this phenomenon on child development, human capital accumulation, and socio-political development. Here we only touch on the first issue.

The most basic point is the extent of inadequate parenting left-behind children receive from a single parent or from their "surrogate parents," who are mostly their grandparents. Let's begin with the left-behind children with both parents absent (narrow definition). As shown in Table 9.5, nearly all (95 percent) children with no parent at home (both parents absent) were taken care of by paternal and maternal grandparents. 37 percent of the caregivers were over 60 years old and they tended to have low education and poor health. Although we have every reason to believe that the grandparents would do their best to care for their grandchildren as surrogate parents, they tend not to possess parenting skills that would foster a nurturing and stimulating environment for the left-behind children. Our examination of children's family functions and parental behavior in Chapter 7 also pointed to the inadequacy of caregiver involvement in child early development and inappropriate parenting behavior by caregivers of left-behind children.

It is also worth noting that the caregivers of children with one parent absent had different characteristics depending on whether that absent parent was the mother or the father. Over 95 percent of the children with only father absent were taken care of by their mothers, whereas only three-fourths of caregivers of children with only mother absent were their fathers and the rest were paternal grandparents. This difference explains why the caregivers of children with only mother absent were generally older, less educated, and had poorer physical and mental health than the caregivers of children with either father or no parent absent. Thus, children with both parents absent were likely to be the most vulnerable, and left-behind children with mother absent were more likely to be at risk than those with father absent.

Limited research exists on the factors influencing the mothers' decision to migrate and leave their children behind at a very young age. According to a recent ethnographic study (Liu and Erwin 2015), most migrant women were aware of the distress felt by their left-behind children and the burden on grandparents as caregivers. However, migration was seen as necessary for the family to earn an income that would raise the family living standards, help pay for their children's schooling, and improve their children's life chances.

Yet the toll of leaving children behind on the children's intellectual development and mental and psychological health is a real one. In Chapter 5 we touched on the emotional impact of parental absence on

Table 9.5 Characteristics of primary caregivers of all children by living arrangements (%)

Children's primary caregiver	Living arrangements: parent presence or absence				
	Both parents absent	Father absent	Mother absent	Both parent present	Total
Relation to children *					
Mother	0.4	95.7	0.0	90.6	76.5
Father	0.1	0.4	77.5	6.7	7.3
Paternal grandparents	80.6	2.9	22.3	2.5	13.4
Maternal grandparents	13.7	1.1	0.2	0.2	2.1
Other	5.2	0.0	0.0	0.0	0.7
Caregivers' age *					
16–25	0.2	12.3	2.9	7.8	7.2
26–35	0.9	41.5	22.0	42.9	36.6
36–45	2.6	38.5	41.5	42.6	36.9
46–60	59.0	5.8	22.6	5.4	13.0
Over 60	37.4	2.0	11.1	1.2	6.3
Caregivers' education *					
Less than high school	96.3	85.3	86.1	82.5	84.7
High school	3.7	14.7	13.9	17.5	15.3
Have chronic disease *	18.6	9.6	14.9	8.0	9.8
Self-reported health *					
Unhealthy	31.8	14.9	18.5	10.3	14.0
So-so	38.3	36.3	37.6	36.8	37.0
Healthy	29.9	48.8	44.0	52.8	49.1
Feeling severe stress *	22.7	16.3	20.2	13.7	15.4
Total	100	100	100	100	100

Note: 2010 CFPS child sample $N=8{,}990$. Numbers shown are weighted percentages.
* $p < .05$ based on designed-based Pearson chi-square statistic.

children's subjective well-being. Recent studies conducted in China have pointed to the emotional difficulties and attachment problems faced by left-behind children. One empirical study comparing the brain imaging of left-behind children and children of intact families found larger gray matter volumes in multiple brain regions in the former group, reflecting delayed brain development among left-behind children in China (Yang et al. 2015). Other studies found that children and adolescents who were separated from their parents, especially both parents or only mothers, early in childhood had more symptoms of depression and anxiety (Liu, Li, and Ge 2009).

Summary and conclusion

Massive internal migration has been a major feature of the Chinese model of development. As tens of millions of migrant workers seek work opportunities away from home, they have often had to leave their children behind. Whereas we are used to thinking about the decisions migrant workers have had to make in quest of work opportunities while simultaneously caring for their families, in the aggregate the decisions by the migrating parents to leave their children behind appear far less the outcomes of individual agency and autonomy than the forced (and false) choices imposed by a system of institutions and policies designed to protect the status quo. A segmented job market and restricted access to education have prevented them from bringing their spouse and children with them to destination cities (Li and Wan 2014; Ma et al. 2011).

This chapter has presented empirical data on the patterns of internal labor migration as well as patterns of parental absences from the children they love. We also presented data on the caregivers of children in China, with special attention to the caregivers of left-behind children, who are usually the grandparents. All this information underscores the disadvantages left-behind children in China must contend with and point to the potential adverse consequences parental absence poses for the development of left-behind children and for China's human capital and social development. In Chapter 10, we employ statistical models to further analyze the effect of different types of parental absence on child developmental outcomes.

Note

1 The percentages based on children's *hukou* status are similar.

10 Parental absence and child development outcomes

In previous chapters, we examined several domains of child well-being and the family and community conditions for children in China. We saw significant disparities in the well-being of children in rural and urban areas. We also noted the important role of family configuration in child development. We were especially struck by the institutionalized disadvantages facing left-behind children and the children of single/no-parent families.

The relationship between family structure and child development in the US and other developed countries has been well studied. Children of single-parent families due to non-marital births or marital dissolution were found to have lower levels of physical and psychological well-being and educational attainment than children from intact families (Craigie, Brooks-Gunn, and Waldfogel 2012; Hilton and Devall 1998; Lee and McLanahan 2015; Waite 1995; Wen 2008). Parental absence during childhood was found to affect the child's physical and mental health in later life (Amato 1991, 2005; Maier and Lachman 2000). Researchers attribute the disparities in child development to lower levels of family resources available to children in single-parent or surrogate families due to caregivers' low education, family poverty, lack of social support, limited parental time, and parenting stress (McLanahan 2004; Osborne et al. 2012; Thomson, Hanson, and McLanahan 1994).

Parental absence due to parental emigration in search of jobs, either domestic or overseas, is a common experience of children in many developing countries but usually on a much smaller scale than in China. However, the impact of this absence on child development and well-being, especially education, has not been conclusively examined. In Mexico, paternal migration to the US was shown to benefit girls' educational attainment, but domestic migration had no effect (Antman 2011). The author of the study maintains that the sizeable remittance sent home from abroad boosted family investment in their children's education. However, a later study comparing the outcomes of left-behind children of migrant parents from Mexico and Indonesia indicates that in both countries, parental and especial maternal absence due to international migration, had an adverse effect on children's educational attainment (Lu 2014). In the Philippines, children of migrant parents were found to generally do well in grade schools but tended to score less well academically with migrant mothers (Asis 2006; Asis and Ruiz-Marave 2013). This indicates the importance of maternal presence for the academic performance of children.

In the case of China, existing research on the development and wellbeing of left-behind children has also produced ambiguous results. Although emigrant parents seek to provide their left-behind children with a better life and better schooling through remittances, their efforts may not have the desired results (Lu 2012). The potential benefits from remittances are often offset by the social and emotional costs of family separation and interruption. Published studies have noted various adverse consequences of parental absence on domains of child functioning (Wang and Mesman 2015). A number of studies agree on the greater risk to left-behind children for mental health disorders, such as depression, anxiety, loneliness, levels of happiness, and quality of life (Jia and Tian 2010; Jia, Shi, Cao, et al. 2010; Li 2016; Liu, Li, and Ge 2009). In contrast, Zhou et al. (2015) did not find any significant differences on nine indicators of health, nutrition, and educational outcomes between left-behind children and children living with both parents. However, the generalizability of their study is limited by its sample of school children in poor rural areas. The study also did not differentiate between different types of left-behind children in calculating the outcomes.

Scholars have debated the impact of parental absence on children's school performance. Without differentiating among different forms of parental emigration, Chen et al. (2013) found no significant difference in the probability of liking school and college aspirations between left-behind children and the children of intact families in rural communities. When both parents migrate, particularly the absence of mothers, leaving their children behind with grandparents or other relatives, the children's educational performance tends to suffer (Zheng and Wu 2014; Zhou, Murphy, and Tao 2014). The mother's absence tends to have a negative impact on children's school engagement (Wen and Lin 2012;). Li (2016) also reported that left-behind children were more likely to report a decline in their test scores and to be less satisfied with their school performance.

In this chapter, we make use of additional statistical tools to further explore the effects of family configuration and parental absence on child development and well-being. Selected indicators of well-being representing physical health, sense of happiness, psychological health, cognitive development and educational attainment are used as dependent variables.

We differentiate five types of children's living arrangement based on patterns of parental absence. Besides intact families where both parents stay at home, we distinguish children with both parents as migrants, only father as migrant, and only mother as migrant. Parental absence due to parents' death, divorce, or disappearance is counted as a separate category. Besides controlling for children's demographic characteristics such as gender, ethnicity, and age, we will also explore variations of child development across the three regions of China and for families of different social and economic status. To take into account rural and urban disparities in child well-being outcomes, we either include the community type indicator as a covariate in our modeling or analyze the data separately for rural and urban children.

Physical well-being

Childhood sickness is an important indicator of children's physical well-being. In Chapter 4, we learned that the percentage of children aged zero to three who were reported to be sick in the previous month were higher for left-behind children whose parents were both absent from home in 2010 or 2014. In order to examine the validity of the bivariate results, we pool all children aged 0 to 15 from three waves of the CFPS survey (2010, 2012, 2014).

Table 10.1 shows the distribution of living arrangements for rural and urban children and the proportion of children in each category who were reported by their caregivers to be sick in the previous month.[1] Interestingly, for both rural and urban children, those with their fathers absent had the highest morbidity rate. In the case of rural children, however, those children with both parents absent were also more prone to sickness but that's not the case for the similarly situated urban children.

Considering the potentially different effects of parental absence on childhood sickness in urban and rural areas, we analyze the urban and rural children separately using random-effects logistic regression models. The random effects estimates take into account the clustering of some children across the three waves of survey to arrive at robust and efficient estimates. The results of two models each for rural and urban children are shown in Table 10.2. The odds ratio coefficient for

Table 10.1 Percentage of children sick last month by parental absence in rural/urban communities (2010–2014)

Parental absence	Rural communities		Urban communities		Total	
	Frequency	% Sick	Frequency	% Sick	Frequency	% Sick
Both parents absent	2,437	33.3	353	27.2	2,790	32.5
Only father absent	2,399	34.6	405	35.6	2,804	34.7
Only mother absent	517	29.4	81	25.9	598	28.9
Both parents present	13,567	28.5	5,026	29.0	18,593	28.6
Death/divorce of parent	930	30.0	316	27.5	1,247	29.5
Total	19,850	29.9	6,181	29.3	26,032	29.7

Note: Total sample includes all children 0 to 15 years old from 2010, 2012, and 2014 surveys.

a predictor variable shows the ratio of the odds of getting sick for children in that category relative to children in the reference category. An odds ratio of larger than one indicates a higher probability of being sick for children in that category. Covariates in Model 1 include child demographics (gender, ethnicity minority, age, and squared age), geographic region, and survey year. In Model 2, we add the social and economic status (SES) indicators of families (whether the father and mother had high school education and whether the family was in poverty).

The regression results from the different models indicate that the effects of children's demographic attributes on their likelihood of disease are different in rural and urban areas. While both rural and urban children are less likely to report being sick as they grow up, gender matters only in urban areas where boys are more likely to get sick than girls. While children of ethnic minorities report significantly lower probability of sickness than Han children in rural areas, ethnicity makes no difference in urban areas. Across the survey years, children in both 2012 and 2014 are less likely to become sick than in 2010 especially in rural areas. This general improvement in the physical health of children is expected given the major improvements in their economic well-being during the study period.

There are significant differences in the prevalence of childhood sickness across regions. In rural areas, children in both the western and central regions have a significantly lower probability of becoming sick than children in the eastern areas. In urban areas, only children in the western region report a lower probability of sickness than in the eastern region or central region. Considering the lower levels of economic development in the western region, the lower prevalence of child sickness in the west is puzzling and requires further examination in the future.

For family SES indicators, poverty has a major impact only in urban areas, where children in poverty have 1.39 times the odds of getting sick than children not in poverty. In rural areas, children whose mothers have a high school education are less likely to report being sick, while in urban areas it is the father's high school education that has the same effect.

The regression results indicate parental absence has significant effects on children's physical well-being in rural areas. Rural children who live with both parents have a much lower probability of getting sick than children with both parents absent or father absent, or with parents deceased or divorced. The statistical patterns about children in urban areas are far less clear-cut. Urban children with absent fathers tend to have the highest probability of sickness, even when compared to children with both parents absent. Overall, it appears that in urban areas the absence of mothers or of both parents does not pose as serious a problem for children's physical well-being as in rural areas. These are puzzling findings that will require further investigation.

Our analyses highlight the detrimental effect of parental absence on the morbidity of children, especially in rural areas. Although not reported here, our analysis of the association between parental absence and several other physical health indicators such as low birthweight and hospitalization also reinforce the conclusion that, in statistically significant terms, parental absence is associated with decreases in children's physical well-being.

Psychological well-being: sense of happiness

As a major indicator of psychological well-being, the feeling or sense of happiness, has been associated with children's demographic characteristics as well as features of family and social context such as parental migration (Wang and Zou 2010). Our bivariate analysis in Chapter 5 found that children in rural areas were not as happy as those in urban areas. We also noted the adverse effects of parental absence, especially in cases of both parents being away or of parental death/ divorce.

In this section we employ multiple linear regression models to probe into the impact of parental absence on children's psychological

Table 10.2 Random-effects logistic regression for probability of sickness for children in rural and urban communities

Covariates	Rural communities				Urban communities			
	Model 1		Model 2		Model 1		Model 2	
	Odds ratio	Sig.	Odds ratio	Sig.	Odds ratio	Sig.	Odds ratio	Sig.
Child male	1.04		1.04		1.19	*	1.19	*
Child ethnic minority	0.67	***	0.66	***	1.01		1.00	
Child age	0.86	***	0.86	***	0.89	***	0.89	***
Child age squared	1.00	*	1.00	*	1.00		1.00	
Parental absence								
Both parents absent	1.24	***	1.23	***	0.66	*	0.67	*
Father absent	1.22	***	1.21	***	Ref.		Ref.	
Mother absent	1.12		1.12		0.61		0.61	
Both present	Ref.		Ref.		0.80	+	0.82	
Death/divorce of parents	1.33	**	1.33	**	0.93		0.91	
Survey year (ref.=2010)								
2012	0.73	***	0.73	***	0.84	*	0.84	*
2014	0.90	**	0.91	*	0.91		0.92	
Region (ref.=eastern region)								
Central region	0.80	***	0.80	***	1.05		1.04	
Western region	0.83	***	0.82	***	0.86		0.83	+
Father high school			0.97				0.85	*
Mother high school			0.84	**			1.06	
Family in poverty			1.00				1.39	**

Intercept	1.17	*	1.22	**	1.12	1.14
Number of obs.	19,850		19,850		6,181	6,181
Number of children	9,825		9,825		3,554	3,554
Wald chi2 (11)	913.58		921.51		303.32	314.61
Prob. > chi2	<.0001		<.0001		<.0001	<.0001

Note: Analysis include all children (birth to 15) surveyed in 2010, 2012, and 2014 with reports of being sick in the previous month.
Significance: + p <.1, * p <.05, ** p <.01, *** p <.001.

108 *Parental absence and child development*

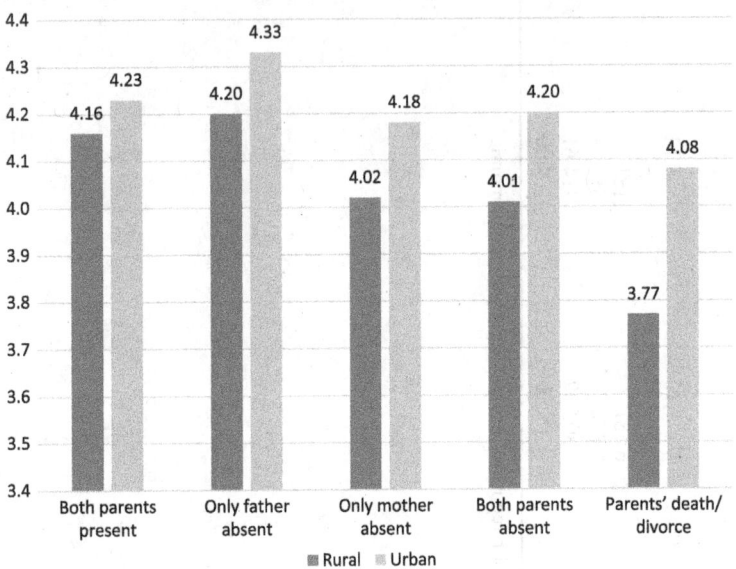

Figure 10.1 Average happiness score by living arrangement and community type

well-being in terms of the sense of happiness. Since in the CFPS surveys only children aged ten or older were asked about their feeling of happiness, our sample include all children ten years old and above who have valid answers on happiness in the 2010, 2012, and 2014 waves of the survey. Because the 2012 and 2014 surveys used the zero to ten-point Likert scale for measurement of happiness instead of the five-point scale used in 2010, we use a linear transformation to rescale the 2012 and 2014 happiness scores to a scale ranging from one to five, with higher values indicating higher levels of happiness. We include as covariates children's demographic characteristics, family poverty level, and caregiver parenting behavior.

Figure 10.1 summarizes the levels of happiness for children in different living arrangements according to community type. The pattern that immediately jumps off the figure is the higher average happiness score for urban vs. rural children for each type of family living arrangement. Meanwhile, for both rural and urban respondents, the pattern of variation in happiness across living arrangement types are similar. Children with both parents at home score well on the happiness measure. However, the children with fathers having migrated away for work, the most populous type of left-behind children, have a higher average happiness score than children in intact families, especially in urban areas. We can speculate on the intra-family dynamics behind this interesting and potentially significant phenomenon and hope to find out more. Not surprisingly, children with both parents absent or only mother absent have lower happiness scores while children who experienced parental death or divorce have the lowest average score, with the rural children clearly the hardest hit.

Table 10.3 presents the results of random-effects GLS regression models on levels of happiness for children/youth aged ten and older in China in 2010, 2012, and 2014. The random-effects estimates are efficient by taking into account the clustering of children across the three waves of the survey. The coefficients for the four categories of parental absence (with both parents absent as the reference) are similar for the first three models. The results from these models indicate that the variables "children with both parents absent" and "children with only mothers absent" have similar effect on the children's sense of happiness. Both groups of left-behind children tend to be significantly less happy than children of intact families or children with only absent fathers. Children whose parents are either dead or divorced are the least happy. The difference of average happiness scores between children with only fathers absent and orphaned or single-parent children is 0.35 (i.e., 0.192-(-0.157)), which is nearly half a standard deviation of the happiness score (M=4.15, SD=0.84).

Although the children in the sample are all ten years old and above, parental absence in their early childhood (before three years old) still appears to have a negative effect on their feelings of happiness. Compared with children whose parents were at home almost all year round, children whose parents were absent for one to six months and for one to two years are less happy.

Studies have shown that positive parenting behavior has beneficial effect on children's subjective well-being by moderating the impact of adverse childhood experiences (Armstrong et al. 2005). In Model 4, we include three indicators of positive parenting behavior, first introduced in Chapter 7, in order to test for the effect of parenting behavior. The results confirm the positive effect of certain types of parenting behaviors on children's happiness. Of the three indicators, parenting behavior characterized by encouragement of children has the most beneficial effect.

The children's levels of happiness also vary with their demographic characteristics. Male children are less happy than females. Ethnic minority children are less happy than the Han. In Model 3, parents'

Table 10.3 Random effects GLS regression estimates of happiness of children and youth in China in 2010, 2012, 2014

Covariates	Model 1		Model 2		Model 3		Model 4	
	Coeff.	Sig.	Coeff.	Sig.	Coeff.	Sig.	Coeff.	Sig.
Child male	−0.111	***	−0.115	***	−0.113	***	−0.123	***
Child ethnic minority	−0.143	***	−0.101	**	−0.082	*	−0.008	
Child age	−0.072	*	0.022		0.019		0.029	
Child age squared	0.002		−0.002	+	−0.002		−0.002	
Parental absence (ref.: both absent)								
Father absent	0.192	***	0.195	***	0.186	***	0.183	**
Mother absent	0.026		0.024		0.014		0.109	
Both parents present	0.144	***	0.132	***	0.122	**	0.185	***
Death/divorce of parents	−0.157	**	−0.186	***	−0.193	***	−0.070	
Survey year (ref.: 2010)								
2012			−0.134	***	−0.135	***	−0.020	
2014			0.154	***	0.155	***	0.127	***
Region (ref.: eastern region)								
Central region			−0.018		−0.017		0.000	
Western region			−0.086	***	−0.081	**	−0.090	**
Urban community			0.084	***	0.029		−0.014	
Father's age (ref. age<=35)								
36 to 45 years					0.058	+	0.052	
46 and older					−0.025		−0.036	
Mother's age (ref. age<=35)								
36 to 45 years					−0.076	**	−0.054	+
46 and older					−0.099	*	−0.068	
Father high school					0.106	***	0.080	*
Mother high school					0.064	*	−0.038	

	Model 1	Model 2	Model 3	Model 4
Family in poverty			−0.042 +	−0.083 **
Parents absent bef. age 3 (ref.:<1 month)				
1 to 6 months			−0.133 *	−0.142 *
6 to 12 months			−0.052	−0.038
1 to 2 years			−0.190 *	−0.148
over 2 years			−0.130	−0.119
Parenting behavior				
Engage				0.034 *
Encourage				0.223 ***
Interact				0.108 ***
Intercept	4.776 ***	4.236 ***	4.242 ***	4.054 ***
Sample size N	10166	10163	10068	4753
R-squared	0.027	0.051	0.057	0.116
Wald Chi2 (prob>chi2)	184.2 ***	504.68 ***	590.43 ***	513.3 ***

Note: Analysis include children (1) surveyed in 2010, and (2) reporting happiness values in any of 2010, 2012, 2014 survey years.
Significance: + p <.1, * p <.05, ** p <.01, *** p <.001.

high school education is positively associated with children's happiness, while family poverty tends to have a dampening effect.

Cognitive development and educational attainment

In Chapter 6, we presented the scores of vocabulary and math tests that were administered to children and youth aged 10–15 and noted the rural-urban disparities in the test scores, with rural males having the lowest average scores. We also discussed how the test scores varied by living arrangements.

In this section, we hope to gain additional insights by further analyzing the child data on test performance in rural and urban areas separately. The data includes all children and adolescents with valid test scores surveyed in CFPS 2010 and 2014. They were 10 to 15 in 2010 and 10 to 19 in 2014 (the 15 year olds of 2010 were 19 in 2014). Since many children were tested in both years, robust clustered estimates are used to adjust for correlation of observations between the two survey years. The results of linear regression models for vocabulary test and math test scores are shown in Tables 10.4 and 10.5 respectively. Model 2 of each regression exercise includes indicators of parenting behavior.

Table 10.4 contains the robust estimates of coefficients from linear regression models on the vocabulary test scores of children in rural and urban areas. Model 1 shows that a number of child individual and family factors are negatively associated with vocabulary test scores for both rural and urban children: males, ethnic minority children, and parents without high school education. Family poverty has a negative impact on vocabulary test scores only for rural children.

The results of Model 1 again remind us of the rural-urban difference in the effect of parental absence. For urban children, the absence of both parents or that of mothers only is negative for the children's vocabulary test scores. In rural areas, the most vulnerable children are those with absent mothers and those with divorced or deceased parents. Children in rural areas with both parents absent do not perform differently from children of intact families or only father absent on the vocabulary test. Model 2 in Table 10.4 confirms the importance of positive parenting styles on child performance on the vocabulary test, with the "encouragement" style being the most impactful.

Table 10.5 does the same for math test scores. In Model 1, we find the individual and family risk factors for math performance: ethnicity minority children, parents without high school education, and rural children in poverty. They are similar to the results for vocabulary test scores except for gender which is no longer significant. Model 2 also

Table 10.4 Linear regression with cluster robust estimates for vocabulary test scores of children and youth in China in 2010 and 2014

Covariates	Urban areas				Rural areas			
	Model 1		Model 2		Model 1		Mode 2	
	Coeff.	Sig.	Coeff.	Sig.	Coeff.	Sig.	Coeff.	Sig.
Child male	−1.16	***	−0.17		−1.20	***	−0.66	*
Child ethnic minority	−1.14	*	0.45		−3.01	***	−2.90	***
Child age	6.27	***	−3.49		5.91	***	2.68	
Child age squared	−0.18	***	0.23		−0.16	***	−0.03	
Parental absence (ref. both absent)								
Father absent	1.68	*	2.35		−0.03		−0.69	
Mother absent	−0.25		1.54		−1.46	*	−2.05	+
Both parents present	1.40	**	2.22	+	−0.26		−0.16	
Death/divorce of parents	1.56	*	2.79	+	−1.10	*	−1.31	
Father's age (ref. age<=35)								
36 to 45 years	0.31		−0.59		0.54	+	0.34	
46 and older	−0.06		1.32		−1.07	*	0.02	
Mother's age (ref. age<=35)								
36 to 45 years	−0.86	*	−0.24		−0.30		−0.69	+
46 and older	−1.17	+	−1.78		−0.75		−2.67	*
Father high school	1.36	***	1.96	**	1.72	***	1.17	*
Mother high school	1.63	***	1.32	*	1.57	**	0.75	
Family in poverty	−0.59	*	−0.21		−1.36	***	−1.62	***
Parents absent before age 3 (ref. <= 1 month)								
1 to 6 months	−0.27		1.63		0.04		−0.14	

(continued)

Table 10.4 (Cont.)

Covariates	Urban areas				Rural areas			
	Model 1		Model 2		Model 1		Model 2	
	Coeff.	Sig.	Coeff.	Sig.	Coeff.	Sig.	Coeff.	Sig.
6 to 12 months	−0.03		0.11		−0.93	*	0.61	
1 to 2 years	−0.70	+	−0.43		−0.75		−1.42	
over 2 years	−0.89		−0.11		−1.45		−1.79	
Survey year (ref.=2010)	0.49		−1.25	+	0.29		0.38	
Region (ref.=eastern region)								
Central region	0.11		−0.13		0.38		−0.66	
Western region	0.33		0.98		−0.44	+	−1.16	**
Parenting behavior								
engage			−0.52				0.00	
encourage			1.27	***			1.27	***
interact			0.25	*			−0.36	
Intercept	−26.86	***	29.45	***	−25.45	***	−4.89	
Sample size N	1733		439		5234		1433	
R-squared	0.316		0.210		0.286		0.196	
Model Fit: F Test	37.3	***	6.21	***	100.09	***	13.95	***

Note: Sample includes children and youth (1) surveyed in 2010 and 2014, and (2) with valid test scores (over ten years old).
Significance: + $p <.1$,
* $p <.05$, ** $p <.01$, *** $p <.001$.

Table 10.5 Linear regression with cluster robust estimates for math test scores of children and youth in China in 2010 and 2014

Covariates	Urban areas				Rural areas			
	Model 1		Model 2		Model 1		Mode 2	
	Coeff.	Sig.	Coeff.	Sig.	Coeff.	Sig.	Coeff.	Sig.
Child male	−0.12		0.50	+	−0.14		0.12	
Child ethnic minority	−0.79	*	0.20		−1.12	***	−0.69	*
Child age	4.75	***	−1.84		3.31	***	1.10	
Child age squared	−0.13	***	0.15		−0.08	***	0.00	
Parental absence (ref.: both absent)								
Father absent	1.79	**	0.57		−0.51	+	−0.02	
Mother absent	0.17		0.60		−0.42		−0.88	
Both parents present	1.24	**	0.75		−0.24		0.12	
Death/divorce of parents	1.36	*	1.00		−0.49		−0.04	
Father's age (ref.: age<=35)								
36 to 45 years	0.04		−0.02		0.06		−0.35	
46 and older	−0.01		0.64		−1.06	***	−0.46	
Mother's age (ref.: age<=35)								
36 to 45 years	−0.36	**	0.37		0.23		0.01	
46 and older	−1.22		0.40		−0.01		−0.14	
Father high school	0.88	***	0.28		1.14	***	0.62	*
Mother high school	0.97	***	0.86	*	1.31	***	0.19	
Family in poverty	−0.55		0.10		−0.72	***	−0.52	
Parents absent before age 3 (ref.: <= 1 month)								
1 to 6 months	−0.60		0.44		−0.45		−0.69	+
6 to 12 months	−0.23		0.40		−0.38		0.09	

(continued)

Table 10.5 (Cont.)

Covariates	Urban areas				Rural areas			
	Model 1		Model 2		Model 1		Mode 2	
	Coeff.	Sig.	Coeff.	Sig.	Coeff.	Sig.	Coeff.	Sig.
1 to 2 years	−1.49	*	−1.71		−0.29		−0.54	
over 2 years	−0.37		−1.94		−0.90		−0.90	
Survey year (ref.: 2010)	0.04		0.34		−0.47		0.61	**
Region (ref.: eastern region)								
Central region	0.05		0.10		0.08		−0.44	
Western region	−0.28		0.13		−0.51	**	−0.77	***
Parenting behavior								
engage			0.20				0.04	
encourage			0.43	*			0.47	***
interact			−0.25				0.01	
Intercept	−28.38	***	9.55		−17.30	***	−3.32	
Sample size N	1734		439		5234		1433	
R–squared	0.456		0.284		0.334		0.178	
Model Fit: F Test	69.61	***	8.14	***	126.92	***	11.38	***

Note: Sample includes children and youth (1) surveyed in 2010 and 2014, and (2) with valid test scores (over ten years old).
Significance: + $p < .1$,
* $p < .05$, ** $p < .01$, *** $p < .001$.

shows that positive parenting behavior is beneficial for children's math test scores, but the effect is weaker than on vocabulary tests.

Unlike the results for vocabulary test scores, parental absence is found to be relevant for math test performance for urban children only. Urban children with both parents absent or with only absent mothers fare worse than the other groups of urban children. This finding is the same as for vocabulary test performance of urban children, which shows the crucial role of mothers in enhancing the cognitive performance of their children (Zheng and Wu 2014). The absence of fathers, paradoxically, appears to be conducive to the children's cognitive performances, a phenomenon we hope to further investigate.

Closely related to cognitive development are the issues of educational opportunity and educational attainment. While educational attainment is an important indicator of the effectiveness of government efforts in human capital investment, we know from Chapter 7 that Chinese parents think they should "take great responsibility for the child's grades at school" and are willing to make sacrifices to provide for their children's education.

As we discussed in Chapter 6, most adolescents without grade retention or schooling interruption finish their nine-year compulsory education and graduate from middle school by age 15 or 16. For the absolute majority of them, they then either join the labor force or attend regular or vocational high school. For a 16-year-old, this is not a simple personal choice but one that is heavily affected by community and family conditions. As can be seen in Chapter 6, a much higher proportion of adolescents in certain types of families e.g., those with parents absent, are not in school and hence are also not likely to attend college compared to youths of intact families.

To examine the effects of various individual and family factors on child educational status, we ran multinomial logistic regression models to analyze the 2014 adolescent data for rural and urban areas separately. The dependent variable for these models is educational status, which includes four categories: not in school, in middle school, in high school, and in college. Most of the adolescents not in school have no high school education; they either did not go to high school or had dropped out.

For the sake of space and exposition, we leave out the tables for this exercise and only highlight some of the findings from the analysis. To begin with, in both rural and urban areas, males and ethnic minority adolescents are more likely to be out of school instead of attending high school. There is no significant variation among the three regions regarding the probability of being out of school. However, rural and urban adolescents in the western region are more likely to be still attending middle school and less likely to be in college compared to those in the eastern region. For both rural and urban adolescents, mother's high school education boosts the children's chances of being in high school. Father's high school education has this effect for only urban adolescents.

Parental absence has a major impact on adolescents' education status in both urban and rural areas. Urban adolescents left behind by both parents are the most susceptible to leaving school rather than attending high school compared to any other groups of urban youth. In rural areas, adolescents have a higher chance of dropping out of school when both parents or their mothers are absent from home.

Conclusion and summary

In this chapter, we presented the results of multiple regression analysis on several major domains of child well-being with special attention to the effect of parental absence. First, the results reinforce the point that parental absence does matter for the well-being of children, including child morbidity, feeling of happiness, cognitive test performance, and educational attainment. This is so even after we adjust for children's demographic characteristics and other family conditions. Second, the effects of parental absence on child well-being are not uniform for different types of parental absence, and also differ for distinct domains of child well-being. For example, children's subjective well-being is adversely affected by both parents' absence or only mother's absence, but not by only the father's absence. The same applies to cognitive tests for urban children, where father absence and both parents present have similar effects. Third, the effects of parental absence differ in rural and urban areas. For vocabulary test performance, death or divorce of parents is a significant risk factor for rural children, but not for children in urban areas. Finally, our findings confirm the importance of positive parenting behavior in promoting child well-being. Caregiver encouragement and support of their children are associated with children's higher level of happiness and help with their cognitive test performances.

Our findings call for further examination of the specific family dynamics, parental roles and parenting practices in different family configurations. Given our discovery of the significance of parenting behavior and recent studies that reveal an absence of modern parenting in rural families and families with migrant parents (Luo et al. 2017; Yue et al. 2017), rural children should benefit from the training of a caregiver in knowledge of child development and proper parenting skills.

Note

1 Although parental absence due to migration mostly occurs in rural areas, some parents in urban communities also migrate to other urban areas, most likely larger cities, for better opportunities.

11 Conclusion

The true measure of any society is how it treats its children, who are in turn that society's future. Making use of data from the China Family Panel Studies (CFPS) survey, the first longitudinal survey of Chinese families, we are privileged to have the opportunity to provide a comprehensive picture of the conditions and welfare of children and youth in contemporary China. CFPS is still young, but its first few waves were conducted in years that marked the height of the China Model, the Chinese transition from hyper to more moderate economic growth, and the transition of the Chinese national leadership from Hu Jintao to Xi Jinping. As a result, we are able to capture, through our descriptions and analyses, how various indicators of China's children and youth have changed, often for the better, amid China's economic boom. We have also sought to shed light on the formable challenges that remain for children as individuals, their families, and for China as a whole.

An oft-quoted saying, often attributed to Mahatma Gandhi, states that "The true measure of any society can be found in how it treats its most vulnerable members." Throughout the volume we have made an effort to delineate various forms of disparities and especially the vulnerabilities of children and youth in fragile families and communities. No other country in the world has managed to keep so many of its families divided on the altar of economic growth for such a long period. We have therefore given special attention to the millions of left-behind children. Yet children and youth are not simply charges to be taken care of but are also stakeholders and potential change agents. To better understand their relationship with the status quo and their potential as agents of change, we present findings on youth attitudes toward various social and political issues and compare them with the attitudes of older cohorts.

In carrying out our research, we have paid attention to how family and community conditions affected children's behavior. We classify Chinese children into different categories in terms of family arrangements that reflect patterns of parental migration and absence. Yet we are also keenly aware of the importance of China's political, social, and economic institutions and policies as well as some megatrends—urbanization, migration, demographic change, and rising educational expectations—that these institutions and policies have shaped. The rural-urban disparity is the most salient social cleavage in China that is sustained by the *hukou* household registration system and other related and often exclusionary policies. As a result of the *hukou* system and other policies, it is difficult for most migrant workers to live and work in the cities and raise their children there. Hence the millions of left-behind children who suffer from parental absence and associated negative consequences on major aspects of child well-being.

In this chapter, we briefly summarize our major findings and their implications. We will also review a number of recent government initiatives and policies bearing on the well-being of children and youth and connect them with our findings and also touch on selected new government initiatives and their prospects, and our thoughts on ways to further the welfare of all children.

What have we found?

In general, there was substantial improvement in the material conditions of children during the study period of 2010 to 2014, as measured by indicators such as access to tap water and a flush toilet, especially in rural areas. The number of children living in poverty dropped for families in all categories while a higher percentage of families received government aid under the Chinese government's poverty alleviation program. Our analysis also reveals positive changes in children's physical health conditions (such as the rate of low birthweight) while health insurance coverage for children in both rural and urban areas increased significantly.

Yet the rural disadvantages have persisted in many aspects. Apart from the generally inferior living conditions and poverty for many children in rural communities, the most vulnerable groups are rural children left behind by both parents, urban migrant children, and orphaned or one-parent children. As of 2014, over 50 percent of zero to three year olds in migrant families and families with both parents away were reported being sick "in the past month." Moreover, obesity has become a growing concern, with over 20 percent of rural children being obese. Significant gaps exist between rural and urban children in their levels of happiness, mental stress and social skills. In addition, children left behind by both parents, children in single-parent families, and orphaned children are especially vulnerable to social and emotional challenges.

The rural urban cleavage is most clearly shown in terms of schooling experience and education attainment. Although pre-school enrollment has greatly increased for rural children aged three to five, it still lags far behind that of urban children. Enrollment in public schools (grades one to nine) is high for both rural and urban children; however, over a third of rural children are boarding at school as a consequence of a push to consolidate schools and close down outlying ones. A much lower proportion of rural adolescents attend high school or go on to college. Among the six family arrangements, children left-behind by both parents and single-parent and orphaned children are more likely to drop out of high school and are less likely to attend college.

The starkest rural-urban disparity lies in the family and community environment in which children grow up. Children in rural areas usually lack a supportive family context characterized by a stimulating home environment, positive parenting behaviors, and caregiver involvement in school work. Children left behind by both parents, usually cared for by their grandparents, fare especially poorly.

The scale of parental migration away from their children in China has been simply astounding in global terms and reflects the structural inequalities the Chinese Party-state has maintained. An examination of patterns of parental migration as well as the timing and duration of parental absence reveals that a large proportion of rural children experienced long periods of parental absence at infancy and toddlerhood. A quarter of the four-year-old children in rural areas were left behind by both parents. The results of our analysis confirm that parental absence, especially the absence of both parents or of mothers, have a significant negative impact on the well-being of children, including morbidity, feeling of happiness, cognitive performance, and educational attainment.

Children who migrate with their parents to urban settings also face many hurdles in gaining equal access to education and other resources. Yet they are China's strivers and, in spite of the various obstacles they and their families must contend with, fare much better on a range of development outcomes than their peers who remain in rural areas. They tend to have better social skills, superior cognitive performance, and higher education attainment.

We also analyzed the social attitudes and values of Chinese youth. Having grown up in a period of sustained prosperity and greater individual choice, the younger Chinese cohorts are more independent in spirit, more open-minded socially, and more critical of government performance. They are significantly less deferential to authority than older cohorts. They tend to accept gender equality values, especially in urban areas. And they also are more likely to see hard work as the route to success. Both urban and rural youth are critical of government performance but urban youth somewhat more so.

Why should we care?

Our analyses underscore the persistence of inequalities along multiple dimensions and especially between rural and urban children in family living conditions, community resources, and parental support and involvement. These inequalities are undergirded and reinforced by a set of institutions and policies centered around the *hukou*. Rural residents may better their economic conditions by migrating to urban areas, but most of them are held down by institutionalized inequalities that make it difficult for them to raise their kids in urban settings as equals with urban kids. For migrant children who are lucky to finish nine years of compulsory education in urban areas, they face the even more formidable barrier of attending local high school and tend to have to return to their parents' hometown to continue schooling or simply stop going to school.

The rural children who were left behind at a younger age and those returning from the urban areas where their parents work—migrant and left-behind children and youths—numbered nearly 100 million in 2015. They have to cope with the emotional strains of extended parental absence, lack of parental supervision, and weak family and community support. With multiple adversities imposed on them, they tend to suffer in their short-term development and be ill-prepared for future opportunities for upward social mobility. Therefore, if not drastically revamped, the current system of structural inequalities will only serve to perpetuate the status quo that channels the new generation of rural children, like their parents, "to the bottom of the urban hierarchy" as an urban underclass of subordinate laborers (Li 2015, 210; Song 2014).

The massive structural inequalities experienced by children, exemplified by the hardships of migrant and left-behind children, may also entail other costs such as increased crime (Yuan 2017) as well as undermine investment in human capital, which is essential to economic growth rate (Barro 2001, 2003). So far Chinese economic growth has relied on abundant but low-skilled labor. As the growth potential of the labor-intensive development model is tapped out, further development will have to become more innovation-based with a well-educated skilled workforce. Compared to many other countries, however, the educational level of China's labor force has been subpar, especially in the interior regions (Li 2017; Wang, Li, and Abbey, et al. 2018). The underinvestment in the education and health of its vulnerable groups of children in China will likely hamper China's prospect of further economic growth and hinder the achievement of its national ambitions.

What is being done?

The findings of this book are closely related to two strands of political and policy developments in China. First, the time period our study covers overlaps with China's Twelfth Five-Year Plan (2011–2015). The changes we find across the 2010 and 2014 survey waves can therefore be used to assess the progress of government efforts on issues relevant to children and youth. Second, after becoming CCP General Secretary in late 2012, Xi Jinping, who also assumed the title of State Chairman (President) in Spring 2013, launched an ambitious China Dream agenda to build "a moderately prosperous society in all respects" by 2020 (Xi 2017). A key initiative of this agenda is to fight against poverty.

These national programs and related measures are expected to affect well-being of Chinese children and youth. In the following, we summarize these efforts and relate them to our concern about child and youth well-being in light of our earlier findings.

Poverty Alleviation and Child Development

A long-standing policy concern, poverty alleviation has risen to the very top of the Chinese government's list of priorities from the Twelfth Five-Year Plan to the Thirteenth Five-Year Plan (2016–2020). President Xi has vowed to lift "all rural residents living below the current poverty line" out of poverty by 2020 (Xinhua 2017). Children living in poverty have been given special attention. In 2016, the Chinese government (State Council) issued guidelines on taking better care of children in difficulty because of family poverty, disabilities, or lack of guardianship (State Council 2016b, 2016c). The guidelines promise public assistance to vulnerable children to help with their basic living conditions, health care needs, education, and guardianship as well as provide welfare services for children with disabilities. Local governments at the county and township levels are asked to build up its service capacity in mandatory reporting, emergency response, needs assessment, service delivery, and the provision of guardianship. Village and urban residents' committees are required to appoint a child welfare director or child rights inspector to learn about the needs of vulnerable children and their families through periodic home visits and help them secure public assistance.

The formal designation of child welfare directors drew on trials conducted with the support of the Ministry of Civil Affairs after 2010. Following the issuance of the State Council guidelines in 2016, the system spread throughout the country quickly. By the end of 2017, there were 127,000 child welfare directors working with vulnerable children at rural and urban communities (China Philanthropy Research Institute and UNICEF 2016; China Philanthropy Research Institute 2018). In many places school teachers have assumed the role as child welfare directors, generally with minimal professional training in child welfare.

Nutrition and health for children are key elements of the State Council's "Plan for the Development of Children in Impoverished Areas" (2014–2020), which calls for various initiatives including disease screening for newborns, nutrition improvement for children, and enhancement of educational resources in impoverished areas (General Office of the State Council 2015). The nutrition improvement program for children in impoverished areas started in 2012 under the leadership of the China Development Research Foundation. To alleviate child malnutrition in impoverished areas, the program provides free nutrition packets for infants and toddlers. As of 2015, 2.57 million children in 341 (designated) poverty counties benefited from the program (CDRF 2017, 62, 67).

Targeted at improving the well-being of vulnerable children and their families, these programs and others have contributed to the official anti-poverty drive. Speaking to the 19th CCP congress, Xi Jinping declared that more than 60 million people had been lifted out of poverty between 2012 to 2017 (Xi 2017). Heading toward 2020, the Chinese leadership has mounted a massive drive to promote "targeted poverty alleviation" (精准扶贫) throughout the country. This drive should benefit disadvantaged children in improving their living environments and physical health conditions (State Council 2016d). However, we need to emphasize that child poverty is multidimensional, and income insecurity is only one of the multiple deprivations facing rural children (Qi and Wu 2014). As the findings in this volume and other studies have shown, inadequate parenting and lack of early childhood education resources are salient issues for child development in rural areas and require effective intervention (Yue et al. 2017).

Pre-school, primary, and secondary education

In addition to poverty alleviation, further improvement in childcare and pre-school education is also expected in China. Our analysis shows that children in rural areas tend to live in a much less stimulating home environment and many experience parental absence at an early age. With parental absence and poor parenting practices by caregivers, pre-school becomes a crucial institution to provide proper care and cognitive stimulation for children, especially left-behind children in rural areas. Yet even in urban areas, parents find it hard to secure access to quality pre-school programs.

Recognizing the twin problems of availability and affordability, the Chinese leadership has made various efforts to promote pre-school education since 2010, both offering some funding and encouraging private providers. The central focus, under the State Council's National Plan of Medium- and Long-term Goals on Education Reform and Development (2010–2020) and "Preschool Three-year Action Plan," has been to raise the pre-school enrollment rate (General Office of the State Council 2010; MOE 2017c; Xinhua 2010) (see Table 11.1).

These efforts, combined with the determination of Chinese families to provide for the education of their offspring, have generated much momentum for expanding pre-school education. According to official statistics, China's pre-school gross enrollment rate reached 77.4 percent in 2016. Our CFPS 2014 sample indicates a 67.5 percent pre-school enrollment rate in 2014, an increase of 12.7 percentage points from 2010. Rural enrollment rose by 16 percentage points to reach 63 percent in 2014 (Chapter 6). To help promote equity in public services, the Chinese government has increased attention to and investment in quality public education for children in rural and poverty stricken areas. Besides increasing government investment in building school facilities and training teachers in rural areas, the Chinese government has implemented the "Two Exemptions and One Subsidy" (两免一补) program that waives tuition and textbook fees and subsidizes boarding cost for students in poverty in rural areas since 2006. Since 2017, the program has expanded to include poor children in urban areas but it is not clear whether it would benefit migrant children attending public schools in urban areas.

Table 11.1 Pre-school education development goals

Target/Year	2009	2015	2020
Number of children in kindergarten (10,000 persons)	2,658	3,400	4,000
Gross admission rate (1 year before school) (%)	74	85	95
Gross admission rate (2 years before school) (%)	65	70	80
Gross admission rate (3 years before school) (%)	51	60	70

Source: Xinhua 2010.

Conclusion 127

Though high school education is not part of government-funded compulsory education, the Chinese government has nonetheless set the target of enrolling over 90 percent of all adolescents and youth in each province in high schools (including vocational and technical schools), up from 87.5 percent in 2016 (MOE 2017b). To boost enrollment in high schools, programs such as the "Rain and Dew Plan" (雨露计划) have been introduced to offer subsidies for vocational trainings to middle and high school graduates from impoverished families (Xinhua 2016; The State Council Leading Group Office of Poverty Alleviation and Development 2007; State Council 2018).

These efforts, combined with the determination of Chinese families to provide for the education of their offspring, have generated much momentum for expanding pre-school education. According to official statistics, China's pre-school gross enrollment rate reached 77.4 percent in 2016. Our CFPS 2014 sample indicates a 67.5 percent pre-school enrollment rate in 2014, an increase of 12.7 percentage points from 2010. Rural enrollment rose by 16 percentage points to reach 63 percent in 2014 (Chapter 6).

Urbanization, hukou reform, and the welfare of children affected by migration

As we have stated repeatedly, a major characteristic of China's development and urbanization is how inequality between rural and urban areas and between urban residents and non-local migrants are sustained and reinforced by the *hukou* system and associated policies. The plight of migrant children and left-behind children can be largely attributed to the discriminatory policies instituted by many municipal authorities to limit non-local students' access to urban education resources.

The Chinese central government directly reviews and approves master plans of the major municipalities, which include targets for the number of residents. Recognizing that urbanization goes hand in hand with development, the central authorities have laid out a vision for growing the number of urban residents in a controlled manner. In the Thirteenth Five-Year Plan (2016–2020) and the New Urbanization Plan (2014–2020), it was indicated that as many of 100 million rural *hukou* residents may gain urban *hukou* by 2020. Many of the *hukou* conversions will likely be due to government-engineered requisition of rural land (Xu, Tang and Chan 2011).

A differentiated population urbanization regime is already in existence among Chinese cities. For small cities with less than half a million residents, migrants can acquire urban *hukou* as long as he or she meet the basic requirements of having a stable residence. Many small and even some middle-sized cities are willing to make their *hukou* available in order to attract property buyers and boost the local economy. In contrast, "megacities," such as Beijing, Shanghai, and Shenzhen, have made it exceedingly difficult for outsiders to gain *hukou* for fear that more population would exacerbate the problem of air pollution, congestion, and water shortage. A "points scheme" has been used to attract more educated or resourceful applicants and keep out others, particularly "low-end population" lacking a college education, thus making most migrants from rural areas ineligible (Xinhua 2015). In winter 2017, Beijing gained notoriety for brutally forcing out tens of thousands of migrant workers in the name of safety (Buckley 2017).

From a children's rights perspective, the population urbanization regime raises questions about China's compliance with the four core principles of the UN Convention on the Rights of the Child, to which China is an early signatory: non-discrimination, best interest of the child, the rights to life, survival and development, and respect for views of the child. The exclusion of migrant children from equal access to urban resources is discriminatory and detrimental to the development of the children. It reinforces the existing social hierarchy and stifles their chance of upward social mobility. It is more than ironic that, despite recent reforms, the Party that seized power in China with peasant support 70 years ago continues to keep in place some of the most discriminatory institutions and practices against rural residents.

Yet the differentiated population urbanization regime will continue to exert an outsized impact on the well-being of children in China, including 34.26 million migrant children and 68.77 million left-behind children (NBS et al. 2017). On the one hand, migrant workers are more likely to move to lower-tier cities where they are more likely to acquire the urban *hukou* and identity. On the other, the megacities are still more attractive destinations for jobs and other opportunities. As the megacities make it difficult for migrant workers to bring their children in tow for education, they essentially force many migrant children to be separated from their parents and be left behind in their hometowns to cope with serious developmental challenges we have documented in this book.

Implications for the future of child and youth well-being in China

While we have highlighted the various disparities in the well-being of China's children and youth, these disparities exist alongside China's massive economic rise and the fact that China's leaders have increasingly turned their attention to fighting against poverty. We expect that the anti-poverty programs, investments in public services such as education and health care, and policies targeting children affected by parental migration and other vulnerable children will help to further improve the well-being of rural children, especially in physical health and education. Yet the urban-rural gap will remain significant, especially because, with urbanization, some of the rural children become urban as their communities get incorporated into the official urban landscape while others acquire urban *hukou* in order to gain access to urban amenities. However, the *hukou* household registration system and associated institutions and policies have proved their staying power and will remain a formidable barrier against efforts to obtain equal rights for migrant children in large cities while smaller cities appear to shift their stance toward attracting outsiders as new residents.

Much remains to be done in China's vast rural areas to build an integrated child welfare system with the resources and manpower to serve the multifaceted needs of vulnerable children and families. The appointment of "child welfare directors" to work with vulnerable children and their caregivers in rural communities are a good start. Among the many duties of the child welfare supervisor are identifying children and families with special needs and teaching parents and caregivers proper parenting skills. Most of these child welfare workers lack professional training in child development or social work, however. There is an urgent need to provide such training and also develop capacities for coordinating the provision and delivery of various professional services to children and families in need.

The benefits of government investment in pre-school programs, especially for children from disadvantaged families, have been well established (Cunha and Heckman 2010; Duncan and Magnuson 2013). Rural children, especially those from left-behind and single/no-parent families, consistently lag behind their urban counterparts in their family environment and parental involvement. High-quality early childhood education programs that incorporate both cognitive and non-cognitive elements in their curriculum can partly make up for the lack of an enriched home environment. Chinese central and local governments have increased the provision of early childhood education in recent years but availability and affordability remain key issues, especially in rural areas.

Besides intervention in early child education, public schools are another major setting where effective measures can be taken to meet the social-emotional needs of rural children. Students, especially those left behind and from single-parent families should benefit from the services of social workers who are trained in school social work and student counseling. They will not only assist students with children's social and emotional difficulties but also make home visits to counsel caregivers in proper parenting. In addition, students in rural schools would also benefit if universal social-emotional learning programs are incorporated into their learning experiences (Durlak et al., 2011).

There is growing recognition in China of the importance of investing in children's future and of helping the less advantaged. Initiatives and policies adopted by national and local authorities in recent years, combined with the efforts to millions of families, have produced substantial improvements in child and youth well-being in China in a time of growing economic prosperity. Strong political commitment is needed to sustain and broaden these improvements and to improve their effectiveness, especially because local authorities facing competing demands from many directions may waver in their efforts.

Bibliography

21st Century Education Institute. 2013. *Where Will Rural Education Go? Review and Reflection on the School Consolidation Policy in Rural Areas* (农村教育向何处去？对农村撤点并校政策的评价与反思). Beijing: Beijing Institute of Technology Press.

Abdel-Khalek, Ahmed. 2006. "Measuring Happiness with a Single-Item Scale." *Social Behavior and Personality: an international journal* 34 (2): 139–150.

All-China Women's Federation (ACWF). 2013. "Report on Rural Left-behind and Rural-Urban Migrant Children in China (中国农村留守儿童、城乡流动儿童状况研究报告)." *Chinese Women's Movement* 2013 (6): 30–34. Retrieved from: http://news.china.com.cn/txt/2013-05/18/content_28862083.htm.

All-China Women's Federation (ACWF). 2015. "China National Program for Child Development (2011–2020)." Retrieved from: www.womenofchina.cn/womenofchina/html1/source/1502/997-1.htm.

Amato, Paul R. 1991. "Parental Absence During Childhood and Depression in Later Life." *The Sociological Quarterly* 32 (4): 543–556.

Amato, Paul R. 2005. "The Impact of Family Formation Change on the Cognitive, Social, and Emotional Well-being of the Next Generation." *The Future of Children* 14 (2): 75–96.

Antman, Francisca M. 2011. "International Migration and Gender Discrimination among Children Left Behind." *The American Economic Review* 101 (3): 645–649.

Armstrong, Mary I., Shelly Birnie-Lefcovitch, and Michael T. Ungar. 2005. "Pathways Between Social Support, Family Well Being, Quality of Parenting, and Child Resilience: What We Know." *Journal of Child and Family Studies* 14 (2): 269–281.

Attané, Isabelle. 2002. "China's Family Planning Policy: An Overview of Its Past and Future." *Studies in Family Planning* 33 (1): 103–113. Retrieved from: https://doi.org/10.1111/j.1728-4465.2002.00103.x.

Asis, Maruja M.B. 2006. "Living with Migration." *Asian Population Studies* 2 (1): 45–67. DOI: 10.1080/17441730600700556.

Asis, Maruja M.B., and Cecilia Ruiz-Marave. 2013. "Leaving a Legacy: Parental Migration and School Outcomes Among Young Children in the Philippines." *Asian and Pacific Migration Journal* 22 (3): 349–376.

Bandura, Albert. 1989. "Human Agency in Social Cognitive Theory." *American Psychologist* 44 (9): 1175–1184.

Banister, Judith. 2004. "Shortage of Girls in China Today." *Journal of Population Research* 21 (1): 19–45.

Barro, Robert, J. 2001. "Human Capital and Growth." *American Economic Review* 91 (2): 12–17. DOI: 10.1257/aer.91.2.12.

Barro, Robert, J. 2003. "Determinants of Economic Growth in a Panel of Countries." *Annals of Economics and Finance* 4 (2): 231–274.

Becker, Gary. 1981. *A Treatise on the Family*. Cambridge, MA: Harvard University Press.

Bilibili Bangumi. 2015. "Those Years, Those Rabbits, and Those Stories: Season 1 (那年那兔那些事儿: 第一季)." Bilibili. March 5, 2015. Retrieved from: www.bilibili.com/bangumi/media/md1689/.

Blumenthal, David, and William Hsiao. 2015. "Lessons from the East — China's Rapidly Evolving Health Care System." *New England Journal of Medicine* 372 (14): 1281–1285. Retrieved from: https://doi.org/10.1056/NEJMp1410425.

Booth, Alan, and Paul R. Amato. 2001. "Parental Predivorce Relations and Offspring Postdivorce Well-Being." *Journal of Marriage and Family* 63 (1): 197–212.

Bos, Karen, Charles H. Zeanah, Nathan A. Fox, Stacy S. Drury, Katie A. McLaughlin, and Charles A. Nelson. 2011. "Psychiatric Outcomes in Young Children with a History of Institutionalization." *Harvard Review of Psychiatry* 19 (1): 15–24.

Bradley, Robert H., and Robert F. Corwyn. 2002. "Socioeconomic Status and Child Development." *Annual Review of Psychology* 53 (1): 371–399.

Bradshaw, Jonathan, Bruno Martorano, Luisa Natali, and Chris de Neubourg. 2013. "Children's Subjective Well-Being in Rich Countries." *Child Indicators Research* 6 (4): 619–635. Retrieved from: https://doi.org/10.1007/s12187-013-9196-4.

Breslau, Joshua, Michael Lane, Nancy Sampson, and Ronald C. Kessler. 2008. "Mental Disorders and Subsequent Educational Attainment in a US National Sample." *Journal of Psychiatric Research* 42 (9): 708–716.

Bronfenbrenner, Urie. 1979. "Contexts of Child Rearing: Problems and Prospects." *American Psychologist* 34 (10): 844–850.

Brooks-Gunn, Jeanne. 1997. *Neighborhood Poverty, Volume 1: Context and Consequences for Children*. New York: Russell Sage Foundation.

Buckley, Chris. 2017. "Why Parts of Beijing Look Like a Devastated War Zone." *The New York Times*, November 30, 2017. Retrieved from: www.nytimes.com/2017/11/30/world/asia/china-beijing-migrants.html.

Cai, Fang. 1999. "Spatial Patterns of Migration under China's Reform Period." *Asian and Pacific Migration Journal* 8 (3): 313–327.

Cai, Zhiliang, and Lingxin Kong. 2014. "Plight of and a Way Out for Rural Education in View of the Movement of School Closure and Consolidation (撤点并校运动背景下乡村教育的困境与出路)." *Tsinghua Journal of Education* 35 (2): 114–119.

Centers for Disease Control and Prevention (CDC). 2013. "Mental Health Surveillance Among Children — United States, 2005–2011." Centers for Disease Control and Prevention. May 17. 2018. Retrieved from: www.cdc.gov/mmwr/preview/mmwrhtml/su6202a1.htm?s_cid=su6202a1_w.

Chan, Aris. 2009. *Paying the Price for Economic Development: The Children of Migrant Workers in China*. Hong Kong: China Labour Bulletin.

Chan, Kam Wing, and Will Buckingham. 2008. "Is China Abolishing the Hukou System?" *The China Quarterly* 195: 582–606.

Chan, Kam Wing, and Li Zhang. 1999. "The Hukou System and Rural-Urban Migration in China: Processes and Changes." *The China Quarterly* 160: 818–855.

Chang, Fang, Wenbin Min, Yaojiang Shi, Kaleigh Kenny, and Prashant Loyalka. 2016. "Educational Expectations and Dropout Behavior among Junior High Students in Rural China." *China and World Economy* 24 (3): 67–85.

Chen, Gilad, Stanley M. Gully, and Dov Eden. 2004. "General Self-Efficacy and Self-Esteem: Toward Theoretical and Empirical Distinction between Correlated Self-Evaluations." *Journal of Organizational Behavior* 25 (3): 375–395.

Chen, Lijun, Dali Yang, and Qiang Ren. 2015. *Report on the State of Children in China*. Chicago: Chapin Hall at the University of Chicago. Retrieved from: www.chapinhall.org/wp-content/uploads/Chapin_CFPSReport2016_ENGLISH_FNLweb-1.pdf.

Chen, Wen, Hongli Jiang, and Yunyu Huang. 2009. "Urban Children's Health Insurance: Evolution and Current Situation (城镇儿童医疗保障的演变与发展现况分析)." *Chinese Journal of Health Policy* 2 (2): 18–23.

Chen, Xinxin, Qiuqiong Huang, Scott Rozelle, Yaojiang Shi, and Linxiu Zhang. 2009. "Effect of Migration on Children's Educational Performance in Rural China." *Comparative Economic Studies* 51 (3): 323–343.

Chen, Xiyin. 2000. "Growing Up in a Collectivist Culture: Socialization and Socioemotional Development in Chinese Children." In A.L. Comunian and U.P. Gielen, eds., *International Perspectives on Human Development*. Lengerich, Germany: Pabst Science Publishers, pp. 331–353.

Chen, Yi, Guanghui Li, Yan Ruan, Lying Zou, Xin Wang, and Weiyuan Zhang. 2013. "An Epidemiological Survey on Low Birth Weight Infants in China and Analysis of Outcomes of Full-term Low Birth Weight Infants." *BMC Pregnancy and Childbirth* 13: 242. Retrieved from: http://doi.org/10.1186/1471-2393-13-242.

China Development Research Foundation (CDRF). 2017. *Report on Child Development in China, 2017: Poverty Alleviation and Early Childhood Development* (中国儿童发展报告: 反贫困与儿童早期发展). Beijing: China Development Press.

China Global Television Network. 2018. "Chinese Variety Show Find Cultural Aspiration and Confidence." *Global Times*, June 15, 2018. Retrieved from: www.globaltimes.cn/content/1107157.shtml.

China News Network. 2016. "One Report Thinks of a Way for Beijing's Population Regulation: Raise the Cost of Living, and Force People to Leave (报告支招北京人口调控: 提高居住成本倒逼疏解)." China News Network. September 28, 2016. Retrieved from: www.chinanews.com/sh/2016/09-28/8017924.shtml.

China Philanthropy Research Institute. 2018. *China Child Welfare and Protection Policy Report 2018* (中国儿童福利与保护政策报告2018). Retrieved from: www.bnu1.org/research/yjcg/4126.html.

China Philanthropy Research Institute and UNICEF. 2016. *China Child Welfare Policy Report: Building Protective Child Welfare System* (中国儿童福利政策报告2016). Retrieved from: www.unicef.cn/cn/uploadfile/2016/0606/20160606033950409.pdf.

Chinese Academy of Sciences. 2012. *China Sustainable Development Report 2012* (中国可持续发展战略报告). Beijing: The Science Press. Retrieved from: www.chinanews.com/gn/2012/03-12/3737442.shtml.

Cheng, Shikun, Li Zhifu, Syed M.N. Uddin, et al. 2018. "Toilet Revolution in China." *Journal of Environmental Management* 216: 347–356. Retrieved from: www.sciencedirect.com/science/article/pii/S030147971730912X.

Chu, Weizhong, and Yuhui Zhang. 2012. "The Adverse Effect of School Closure and Consolidation on Rural Compulsory Education (农村义务教育撤点并校负面影响分析)." *Education and Management* 7: 10–12.

Chui, Wing Hong, and Mathew Y.H. Wong. 2016. "Gender Differences in Happiness and Life Satisfaction among Adolescents in Hong Kong: Relationships and Self-Concept." *Social Indicators Research* 125 (3): 1035–1051.

CNNIC. 2017. The 40th China Statistical Report on Internet Development. CNNIC. Retrieved from: www.cnnic.cn/hlwfzyj/hlwxzbg/hlwtjbg/201708/P020170807351923262153.pdf.

Conger, Rand D., Katherine J. Conger, and Monica J. Martin. 2010. "Socioeconomic Status, Family Processes, and Individual Development." *Journal of Marriage and Family* 72 (3): 685–704.

Craigie, Terry-Ann L., Jeanne Brooks-Gunn, and Jane Waldfogel. 2012. "Family Structure, Family Stability and Outcomes of Five-Year-Old Children." *Families, Relationships and Societies* 1 (1): 43–61.

Cui, Duoli. 2012. "Re-Evaluation Is Needed of the Effects of School Closure and Consolidation in Rural Areas (应重新评估农村撤点并校的实效)." *Education Exploration* 3: 86–87.

Cunha, Flavio, and James J. Heckman. 2010. "Investing in Our Young People." *NBER Working Paper* No. 16201. Retrieved from: www.nber.org/papers/w16201.

Dalton, Russell J., and Christian Welzel. 2014. *The Civic Culture Transformed: From Allegiant to Assertive Citizens*. New York, NY: Cambridge University Press.

Darling-Churchill, Kristen E., and Laura Lippman. 2016. "Early Childhood Social and Emotional Development: Advancing the Field of Measurement." *Journal of Applied Developmental Psychology* 45: 1–7.

Derdikman-Eiron, Ruth, Marit S. Indredavik, Grete H. Bratberg, Gunnar Taraldsen, Inger Johanne Bakken, and Matthew Colton. 2011. "Gender Differences in Subjective Well-Being, Self-Esteem and Psychosocial Functioning in Adolescents with Symptoms of Anxiety and Depression: Findings from the Nord-Trøndelag Health Study." *Scandinavian Journal of Psychology* 52 (3): 261–267.

Diez Roux, Ana. 2001. "Investigating Neighborhood and Area Effects on Health." *American Journal of Public Health* 91 (11): 1783–1789.

Ding, Mingxiu. 2012. "The Institutional Barriers to and Protection of School Entry of Migrant Workers' Children (农民工子女随迁入学的制度性障碍与保障)." *Chinese Agricultural Science Bulletin* 28 (2): 157–160.

Dong, Qi, Yanping Wang, and Thomas H. Ollendick. 2002. "Consequences of Divorce on the Adjustment of Children in China." *Journal of Clinical Child and Adolescent Psychology* 31 (1): 101–110.

Dornbusch, Sanford M., Philip L. Ritter, P. Herbert Leiderman, Donald F. Roberts, and Michael J. Fraleigh. 1987. "The Relation of Parenting Style to Adolescent School Performance." *Child Development* 58 (5): 1244–1257. doi:10.2307/1130618.

Duncan, Greg J., and Katherine A. Magnuson. 2013. "Investing in Preschool Programs." *Journal of Economic Perspectives* 27 (2): 109–132.

Dunifon, Rachel. 2013. "The Influence of Grandparents on the Lives of Children and Adolescents." *Child Development Perspectives* 7 (1): 55–60.

Durlak, Joseph A., Roger P. Weissberg, Allison B. Dymnicki, Rebecca D. Taylor, and Kriston B. Schellinger. 2011. "The Impact of Enhancing Students' Social and Emotional Learning: A Meta-Analysis of School-Based Universal Interventions." *Child Development* 82 (1): 405–432.

Eastman, Lloyd E. 1989. *Family, Fields, and Ancestors: Constancy and Change in China's Social and Economic History, 1550–1949*. Oxford: Oxford University Press.

Economy, Elizabeth C. 2018. *The Third Revolution: Xi Jinping and the New Chinese State*. New York, NY: Oxford University Press.

Fan, C. Cindy. 1999. "Migration in a Socialist Transitional Economy: Heterogeneity, Socioeconomic and Spatial Characteristics of Migrants in China and Guangdong Province." *International Migration Review* 33 (4): 954–987.

Fan, Fang, Linyan Su, Mary Kay Gill, and Boris Birmaher. 2010. "Emotional and Behavioral Problems of Chinese Left-behind Children: A Preliminary Study." *Social Psychiatry and Psychiatric Epidemiology* 45 (6): 655–664.

Fan, Ming, and Wenwu Hao. 2011. "Reflection on the 'Three Goals' of Rural School Consolidation: The Case of Shannxi (对农村学校布局调整三个目的的反思：以陕西为例)." *Peking University Education Review* 9 (2): 178–187.

Fan, Shiyun. 2015. "'Song of the Thirteenth Five-Year' Brings Chinese Propaganda Films into a New Era ('神曲'《十三五之歌》将中国的宣传片带进新时代)."

The Paper, October 28, 2015. Retrieved from: www.thepaper.cn/newsDetail_forward_1390134.

Fan, Xianzuo, and Qingyang Guo. 2009. "School Consolidation in Rural Primary and Secondary Schools: Effects, Problems and Countermeasures (我国农村中小学布局调整的成效、问题与对策)." *Educational Research* 348: 31–38.

Fang, Liang, and Yin Liu. 2013. "Closure and Consolidation of Rural Primary Schools: An Analysis of Accomplishments and Dilemmas (农村小学撤点并校的成效与困境分析)." *Journal of Southwest Petroleum University (Social Sciences Edition)* 15 (3): 36–41.

Fantuzzo, John, Christine McWayne, and Marlo A. Perry. 2004. "Multiple Dimensions of Family Involvement and Their Relations to Behavioral and Learning Competencies for Urban, Low Income Children." *School Psychology Review* 33 (4): 467–480.

Faure, David. 2007. *Emperor and Ancestor: State and Lineage in South China.* Stanford, CA: Stanford University Press.

Festini, Filippo, and Maurizio de Martino. 2004. "Twenty-Five Years of the One Child Family Policy in China." *Journal of Epidemiology and Community Health* 58(5): 358–360.

Fish, Eric. 2015. *China's Millennials: the Want Generation.* Lanham, MD: Rowman & Littlefield.

Fong, Vanessa L. 2002. "China's One-Child Policy and the Empowerment of Urban Daughters." *American Anthropologist* 104 (4): 1098–1109.s

Fong, Vanessa L. 2006. *Only Hope: Coming of Age under China's One-Child Policy.* Stanford, CA: Stanford University Press.

Frankenberg, Erica, Genevieve Siegel-Hawley, and Jia Wang. 2011. "Choice without Equity: Charter School Segregation." *Educational Policy Analysis Archives* 19 (1). Retrieved from http://epaa.asu.edu/ojs/article/view/779.

Freire, Teresa, and Gabriela Ferreira. 2018. "Health-Related Quality of Life of Adolescents: Relations with Positive and Negative Psychological Dimensions." *International Journal of Adolescence and Youth* 23 (1): 11–24.

Gao, Yabing. 2008. "Research on Mental Health and Personality Traits of Rural Children without Parental Care." *Chinese Journal of Public Health* 24 (8): 917–919.

Garces, Eliana, Duncan Thomas, and Janet Currie. 2002. "Longer-Term Effects of Head Start." *American Economic Review* 92 (4): 999–1012.

Geary, David C., Christine Bow-Thomas, Liu Fan, and Robert Siegler. 1993. "Even Before Formal Instruction, Chinese Children Outperform American Children in Mental Addition." *Cognitive Development* 8 (4): 517–529.

General Office of the State Council. 2010. "State Council Opinions on Developing Preschool Education in the Present Time (国务院关于当前发展学前教育的若干意见)." November 24, 2010. Retrieved from: www.gov.cn/zwgk/2010-11/24/content_1752377.htm.

General Office of the State Council. 2015. "Circular of the State Council General Office on Circulating the National Development

Plan for Children in Nationally-designated Poor Areas (2014–2020) [国务院办公厅关于印发国家贫困地区儿童发展规划(2014—2020年)的通知]." Gov.cn. January 15, 2015. Retrieved from: www.gov.cn/zhengce/content/2015-01/15/content_9398.htm.

Guangxi News Net. 2018. "Poor Students in Vocational Schools Can Also Be Nourished by 'Rain and Dew' and Receive 3,000 Yuan in Scholarship Support per Year (贫困中职生也能获"雨露"滋润 每年可获三千助学金)." Gxnews.com.cn. May 9, 2018. Retrieved from: www.gxnews.com.cn/staticpages/20180509/newgx5af23322-17294431.shtml.

Guo, Yuhua, and Binhuan Huang. 2014. "Chinese Characteristics of the World Factory: Sociological Overview of the State of Workers in the New Era (世界工厂的 '中国特色' 新时期工人状况的社会学鸟瞰)." *Chinese Journal of Sociology* 34 (4): 49–55.

Hadfield, Kristin, Margaret Amos, Michael Ungar, Julie Gosselin, and Lawrence Ganong. 2018. "Do Changes to Family Structure Affect Child and Family Outcomes? A Systematic Review of the Instability Hypothesis." *Journal of Family Theory and Review* 10 (1): 87–110.

Hajloo, Nader. 2014. "Relationships between Self-Efficacy, Self-Esteem and Procrastination in Undergraduate Psychology Students." *Iranian Journal of Psychiatry and Behavioral Sciences* 8 (3): 42.

Halman, Loek. 2009. "Political Values." In *The Oxford Handbook of Political Behavior*, by Russell J. Dalton and Hans-Dieter Klingemann, 305–322. New York: Oxford University Press.

Hamoudi, Amar, Desiree W. Murray, L. Sorensen, and A. Fontaine. 2015. "Self-Regulation and Toxic Stress: A Review of Ecological, Biological, and Developmental Studies of Self-Regulation and Stress." *OPRE Report* 30.

Han, Jin, Qingxia Zhao, and Mengnan Zhao. 2016. "China's Income Inequality in the Global context." *Perspectives in Science* 7: 24–29.

Handlin, Oscar. 2002. *The Uprooted: The Epic Story of the Great Migrations that Made the American People*. Philadelphia: University of Pennsylvania Press.

Hannum, Emily C., Meiyan Wang, Jennifer H. Adams. 2008. "Urban-Rural Disparities in Access to Primary and Secondary Education Under Market Reform." In Whyte, Martin K., ed. *One Country, Two Societies? Rural-Urban Inequality in Contemporary China*. Boston, MA: Harvard University Press.

Hanser, Amy. 2002. "Youth Job Searches in Urban China: The use of social connections in a changing labor market." in Gold, Thomas, Doug Guthrie, and David Wank, eds. *Social Connections in China: Institutions, Culture, and the Changing Nature of Guanxi*, 137–161. New York: Cambridge University Press.

Hayslip Jr, Bert, and Patricia L. Kaminski. 2005. "Grandparents Raising Their Grandchildren: A Review of the Literature and Suggestions for Practice." *The Gerontologist* 45 (2): 262–269.

Heckman, James J. 2012. *Giving Kids a Fair Chance*. Cambridge, MA: MIT Press.

Heckman, James, Rodrigo Pinto, and Peter Savelyev. 2013. "Understanding the Mechanisms through Which an Influential Early Childhood Program Boosted Adult Outcomes." *American Economic Review* 103 (6): 2052–2086.

Henrich, Christopher C., and Dana M. Gadaire. 2008. "Head Start and Parental Involvement." *Infants and Young Children* 21 (1): 56–69.

Hilton, Jeanne M., and Esther L. Devall. 1998. "Comparison of Parenting and Children's Behavior in Single-Mother, Single-Father, and Intact Families." *Journal of Divorce and Remarriage* 29 (3–4): 23–54.

Hong, Xiumin, Peng Liu, Qun Ma, Xin Luo. 2015. "The Way to Early Childhood Education Equity – Policies to Tackle the Urban-rural Disparities in China." *International Journal of Child Care and Education Policy* 9: 5. Retrieved from: https://doi.org/10.1186/s40723-015-0008-9.

Huang, Yanzhong, and Dali L. Yang. 2004. "Population Control and State Coercion in China." In Barry Naughton and Dali Yang, eds. *Holding China Together: Diversity and National Integration in the Post-Deng Era*, 193–225. New York, NY: Cambridge University Press.

Hu, Bi Ying, Sherron Killingsworth Roberts, Sylvia Sao Leng Ieong, and Haiying Guo. 2016. "Challenges to Early Childhood Education in Rural China: Lessons from the Hebei Province." *Early Child Development and Care* 186 (5): 815–831.

Hu, Ming, Xiaoyi Fang, Xiuyun Lin, and Yang Liu. 2008. "The Mobility and Social Anxiety of Migrant Children in Beijing and Their Effect on Loneliness (北京流动儿童的流动性, 社交焦虑及对孤独感的影响)." *Applied Psychology* 2: 166–176.

Hu, Yang, and Jacqueline Scott. 2016. "Family and Gender Values in China: Generational, Geographic, and Gender Differences." *Journal of Family Issues* 37 (9): 1267–1293.

Huang, Guoying, and Yu Xie. 2013. "Chapter 5. Cognitive Ability." In Xie, Yu, Xiaopo Zhang, Jianxin Li, Xuejun Yu, and Qiang Ren. *Report on People's Well-being and Development in China, 2013* (中国民生发展报告2013). Beijing: Beijing University Press.

Huang, Yanping, and Ling Li. 2007. "Comparing the Mental Health Status of Different Types of Left-behind Children (不同留守类型儿童心理健康状况比较)." *China Mental Health Journal* 21 (10): 669–671.

Huang, Yukon. 2017. *Cracking the China Conundrum: Why Conventional Economic Wisdom Is Wrong*. 1st edition. New York, NY: Oxford University Press.

Inglehart, Ronald. 1971. "The Silent Revolution in Europe: Intergenerational Change in Post-industrial Societies." *American Political Science Review* 65 (4): 991–1017.

Inglehart, Ronald. 2007. "Postmaterialist Values and the Shift from Survival to Self-Expression Values." In *The Oxford Handbook of Political Behavior*, by Russell J. Dalton and Hans-Dieter Klingemann, 223–239. Oxford: Oxford University Press.

Inglehart, Ronald, and Christian Welzel. 2005. *Modernization, Cultural Change, and Democracy: The Human Development Sequence*. New York, NY: Cambridge University Press.

Ip, Stanley, Mei Chung, Gowri Raman, Priscilla Chew, Nombulelo Magula, Deirdre DeVine, Thomas Trikalinos, and Joseph Lau. 2007. "Breastfeeding and Maternal and Infant Health Outcomes in Developed Countries." *Evidence Report/Technology Assessment No. 153*, AHRQ Publication No. 07-E007. Rockville, MD: Agency for Healthcare Research and Quality. April 2007.

Jankowiak, William R., and Robert L. Moore. 2017. *Family Life in China*. Cambridge, UK: Polity Press.

Jia, Zhaobao, Lizheng Shi, Yang Cao, James Delancey, and Wenhua Tian. 2010. "Health-Related Quality of Life of 'Left-behind Children': A Cross-Sectional Survey in Rural China." *Quality of Life Research* 19 (6): 775–780.

Jia, Zhaobao, and Wenhua Tian. 2010. "Loneliness of Left-behind Children: A Cross-Sectional Survey in a Sample of Rural China." *Child: Care, Health and Development* 36 (6): 812–817.

Ji'nan Municipal People's Government. 2017. "Implementation Opinions of Ji'nan Municipal People's Government on Further Deepening the Reform of the Household Registration System (济南市人民政府关于进一步深化户籍制度改革的实施意见)." August 1, 2017. Retrieved from: www.jinan.gov.cn/art/2017/8/11/art_23034_1011.html.

Kaye-Tzadok, Avital, Sun Suk Kim, and Gill Main. 2017. "Children's Subjective Well-Being in Relation to Gender—What Can We Learn from Dissatisfied Children?" *Children and Youth Services Review* 80: 96–104.

Ke, Mengyuan, Lu Xu, and Xiuxian Zhang. 2015. "School Consolidation Exacerbates the Hollowing Out of Education in Rural Areas (撤点并校加剧农村教育空心化)." *Knowledge Economy* 5: 27–28.

Kessler, Ronald C., Gavin Andrews, Lisa J. Colpe, Eva Hiripi, Daniel K. Mroczek, S.-LT Normand, Ellen E. Walters, and Alan M. Zaslavsky. 2002. "Short Screening Scales to Monitor Population Prevalences and Trends in Non-Specific Psychological Distress." *Psychological Medicine* 32 (6): 959–976.

Kessler, Ronald C., Jennifer Greif Green, Michael J. Gruber, Nancy A. Sampson, Evelyn Bromet, Marius Cuitan, Toshi A. Furukawa, Oye Gureje, Hristo Hinkov, and Chi-Yi Hu. 2010. "Screening for Serious Mental Illness in the General Population with the K6 Screening Scale: Results from the WHO World Mental Health (WMH) Survey Initiative." *International Journal of Methods in Psychiatric Research* 19 (S1): 4–22.

Khor, Niny, Lihua Pang, Chengfang Liu, Fang Chang, Di Mo, Prashant Loyalka, and Scott Rozelle. 2016. "China's Looming Human Capital Crisis: Upper Secondary Educational Attainment Rates and the Middle-income Trap." *The China Quarterly* 228: 905–926.

Kiernan, Kathleen E., and Fiona K. Mensah. 2011. "Poverty, Family Resources and Children's Early Educational Attainment: The Mediating Role of Parenting." *British Educational Research Journal* 37 (2): 317–336.

Knight, John, Lina Song, and Ramani Gunatilaka. 2009. "Subjective Well-Being and Its Determinants in Rural China." *China Economic Review* 20 (4): 635–649. Retrieved from: https://doi.org/10.1016/j.chieco.2008.09.003.

Kramer, M.S. 1987. "Determinants of Low Birth Weight: Methodological Assessment and Meta-analysis." *Bulletin of the World Health Organization* 65 (5): 663–737.

Lai, Fang, Elisabeth Sadoulet, and Alain De Janvry. 2011. "The Contributions of School Quality and Teacher Qualifications to Student Performance Evidence from a Natural Experiment in Beijing Middle Schools." *Journal of Human Resources* 46 (1): 123–153.

Lei, Wanpeng. 2010. "The Spatial Distribution of Compulsory Education Schools(义务教育学校布局)." *Journal of Huazhong Normal University (Humanities and Social Sciences Edition)* 49 (5): 155–160.

Lee, Dohoon, and Sara McLanahan. 2015. "Family Structure Transitions and Child Development: Instability, Selection, and Population Heterogeneity." *American Sociological Review* 80 (4): 738–763.

Leung, Janet T.Y., and Daniel T.L. Shek. 2011. "'All I Can Do for My Child'– Development of the Chinese Parental Sacrifice for Child's Education Scale." *International Journal on Disability and Human Development* 10 (3): 201–208.

Li, Bai, Peymané Adab, and Kar Keung Cheng. 2015. "The Role of Grandparents in Childhood Obesity in China: Evidence From a Mixed Methods Study." *International Journal of Behavioral Nutrition and Physical Activity* 12 (1): 91.

Li, Bai, Rong Lin, Wei Liu, Jingyi Chen, Weijia Liu, Kar Keung Cheng, Miranda Pallan, Peymane Adab, Laura Jones. 2017. "Differences in Perceived Causes of Childhood Obesity between Migrant and Local Communities in China: A Qualitative Study." *PLoS One* 12 (5): e0177505.

Li, Haizheng. 2017. *Report on Human Capital in China in 2017* (中国人力资本报告2017). Beijing: Central University of Finance and Economics. Retrieved from: http://humancapital.cufe.edu.cn/en/2.Human-Capital-Report-Full-Text-Chinese-Version.pdf.

Li, Hongbin, Prashant Loyalka, Scott Rozelle, Binzhen Wu, and Jieyu Xie. 2015. "Unequal Access to College in China: How Far Have Poor, Rural Students Been Left Behind?" *The China Quarterly* 221: 185–207.

Li, Miao. 2015. *Citizenship Education and Migrant Youth in China: Pathways to the Urban Underclass*. Routledge.

Li, Panqiang, Erqin Zeng, and Guohui Yang. 2012. "Between Equity and Efficiency: Investigation into and Reflections on the Closure and Consolidation of Rural Primary and Secondary Schools in the Central Region (公平与效益的博弈：关于中部地区农村中小学撤点并校的调查与反思)." *Journal of Hunan Institute of Humanities, Science and Technology* 4: 103–108.

Li, Shi, and Haiyuan Wan. 2014. "Institutional Labor Market Segmentation in China." *Business and Public Administration Studies* 8 (1): 7–24. Retrieved from: www.bpastudies.org/bpastudies/article/view/183/346.

Li, Xiaowei, and Jing Xie. 2017. "Parenting Styles of Chinese Families and Children's Social-Emotional and Cognitive Developmental Outcomes." *European Early Childhood Education Research Journal* 25(4): 637–650. DOI: 10.1080/1350293X.2017.1331077.

Li, Yan. 2017. "A Recap of 'Clearing the Low-End Population' in Beijing (复盘北京'清退低端人口'始末)." *FT Chinese*. December 12, 2017.

Li, Yifei. 2016. *Whitepaper on Mental Conditions of Left-behind Children in China* (中国留守儿童心灵状况白皮书 2016年). Retrieved from: https://docs.zoho.com.cn/file/jw8rlf2165fc4ceae4e47898d4f3e843e3ef4.

Linver, Miriam R., Jeanne Brooks-Gunn, and Dafna E. Kohen. 2002. "Family Processes as Pathways from Income to Young Children's Development." *Developmental Psychology* 38 (5): 719–734.

Liu, Chengfang, Linxiu Zhang, Renfu Luo, Scott Rozelle, Brian Sharbono, and Yaojiang Shi. 2009. "Development Challenges, Tuition Barriers, and High School Education in China." *Asia Pacific Journal of Education* 29 (4): 503–520.

Liu, Xianchen, Chuanqin Guo, Masko Okawa, Jing Zhai, Yan Li, Makoto Uchiyama, Jenae M. Neiderhiser, and Hiroshi Kurita. 2000. "Behavioral and Emotional Problems in Chinese Children of Divorced Parents." *Journal of the American Academy of Child and Adolescent Psychiatry* 39 (7): 896–903.

Liu, Yunde, Shengjin Wang, Hao Yin, and Qingzhong Gu. 1988. "A Comparative Study of Only-Children and Children with Siblings in China (独生子女与非独生子女比较研究调查报告)." *Population Journal* 3: 17–21.

Liu, Yuzhen, and Lorna Erwin. 2015. "Divided Motherhood: Rural-to-Urban Migration of Married Women in Contemporary China." *Journal of Comparative Family Studies* 46 (2): 241–263.

Liu, Zhengkui, Xinying Li, and Xiaojia Ge. 2009. "Left Too Early: The Effects of Age at Separation from Parents on Chinese Rural Children's Symptoms of Anxiety and Depression." *American Journal of Public Health* 99 (11): 2049–2054.

Lu, Ming. 2016. *Big Country, Big City* (大国大城). Shanghai: Shanghai People's Press.

Lu, Ming, and Yiran Xia. 2016. "Migration in the People's Republic of China." ADBI Working Paper 593. Tokyo: Asian Development Bank Institute. Retrieved from: www.adb.org/publications/migration-people-republic-china/.

Lu, Ping, and Xie Yu. 2013. "China Family Panel Studies: Sampling Weights Calculation for the 2010 Baseline Survey (Second Edition) (中国家庭追踪调查2010年基线调查权数计算[第二版])". *Technical Report Series: CFPS-17*. Beijing: Institute of Social Science Survey, Peking University.

Lu, Yao. 2012. "Education of Children Left Behind in Rural China." *Journal of Marriage and Family* 74 (2): 328–341.

Lu, Yao. 2014. "Parental Migration and Education of Left-Behind Children: A Comparison of Two Settings." *Journal of marriage and the family* 76 (5): 1082–1098.

Luo, Xiaoming. 2005. "A Survey of the Basic Health Situation of Students in Schools for Migrant Children in Economically Developed Areas (经济发达地区流动人口子女学校学生基本健康状况调查)." *Anthology of Medicine* 24 (6): 890–891.

Luo, Renfu, Fang Jia, Ai Yue, Linxiu Zhang, Qijia Lyu, Yaojiang Shi, Meredith Yang, Alexis Medina, Sarah Kotb, and Scott Rozelle. 2017. "Passive Parenting and its Association with Early Child Development." *Early Child Development and Care*, DOI: 10.1080/ 03004430.2017.1407318.

Luster, Tom, and Lynn Okagaki. 2006. *Parenting: An Ecological Perspective.* London and New York: Routledge.

Ma, Jiahong, Chunmei Lu, and Liang Li. 2011. "Analysis of the Accomplishments and Problems of the New Round of Spatial Consolidation of Rural Primary and Secondary Schools: Investigations and Reflections Based on Investigation in Guangxi (新一轮农村中小学布局调整的成效与问题分析: 基于广西的调查与思考)." *Journal of Guangxi Normal University (Philosophy and Social Sciences Edition)* 47 (2): 89–93.

Ma, Rui, Zhigang Xu, Huanguang Qiu, and Junfei Bai. 2011. "Analysis of Factors Affecting the Job Mobility, City Change, and Spouse Companionship of Migrant Workers from Rural Areas (农村进城就业人员的职业流动、城市变换和家属随同状况及影响因素分析)." *China Rural Survey* 2011 (1): 2–9.

Ma, Yanyun. 2009. "Impact of Class Size on Student Performance in Compulsory Education (班额对基础教育阶段学生的影响)." *Educational Science Research* 7: 45–49.

MacFarquhar, Roderick. 2015. "The Superpower of Mr. Xi," New York Review of Books. Retrieved from: www.nybooks.com/articles/2015/08/13/china-superpower-mr-xi/.

Maier, E. Hailey, and Margie E Lachman. 2000. "Consequences of Early Parental Loss and Separation for Health and Well-being in Midlife." *International Journal of Behavioral Development* 24 (2): 183–189.

McLanahan, Sara. 2004. "Diverging Destinies: How Children Are Faring Under the Second Demographic Transition." *Demography* 41 (4): 607–627.

McLanahan, Sara, Laura Tach, and Daniel Schneider. 2013. "The Causal Effects of Father Absence." *Annual Review of Sociology* 39: 399–427.

Meng, Shuchen, Yong Tao, and Jiayi Liu. 2004. "Rural Water Supply and Sanitation in China: Scaling Up Service for the Poor." Retrieved from: http://web.worldbank.org/archive/website00819C/WEB/PDF/CHINA_RU.PDF.

Ministry of Education (MOE). 2012. "Interim Measures for Monitoring and Assessing the Balanced Development of Quality Compulsory Education within Counties (县域义务教育优质均衡发展督导评估办法)." Retrieved from: www.gov.cn/xinwen/2017-05/23/content_5196093.htm.

Ministry of Education (MOE). 2017a. "Work Report on the Work of Monitoring and Assessing the Balanced Development of Quality Compulsory Education in China in 2017 (2017年全国义务教育均衡发展督导评估工作报告)." Retrieved from: www.moe.gov.cn/jyb_xwfb/xw_fbh/moe_2069/xwfbh_2018n/xwfb_20180227/sfcl/201802/t20180227_327990.html.

Ministry of Education (MOE). 2017b. "Program for Achieving the Universalization of High School Education (2017–2022) "高中阶段教育普及攻坚计划 (2017–2020年)."

Ministry of Education (MOE). 2017c. "Statements of the Ministry of Education and Another Three Ministries on Implementing the Third Phase of the Pre-School Education Action Plan (教育部等四部门关于实施第三期学前教育行动计划的意见)." Retrieved from: www.moe.edu.cn/srcsite/A06/s3327/201705/t20170502_303514.html.

Ministry of National Defense. 2018. "'Those Years, Those Rabbits, Those Stories' Special Episode of Zhurihe, Man Guangzhi Becomes 'That Rabbit' (《'那年那兔那些事儿》朱日和篇: 满广志变'那兔')." Gov.cn. January 2, 2018. Retrieved from: www.mod.gov.cn/v/2018-01/02/content_4801296.htm.

Moore, Kristin A., Christina Theokas, Laura Lippman, Margot Bloch, Sharon Vandivere, and William O'Hare. 2008. "A Microdata Child Well-being Index: Conceptualization, Creation, and Findings." *Child Indicators Research* 1 (1): 17–50.

Mullainathan, Sendhil, and Eldar Shafir. 2014. *Scarcity: The New Science of Having Less and How It Defines Our Lives.* New York, NY: Picador.

Naftali, Orna. 2009. "Empowering the Child: Children's Rights, Citizenship and the State in Contemporary China." *The China Journal* 61: 79–103.

National Bureau of Statistics (NBS). 2010. "Administrative Division Codes and Urban-Rural Classification Codes for Statistics (2010 年统计用区划代码和城乡划分代码)." Retrieved from: www.law-lib.com/law/law_view.asp?id=315638.

National Bureau of Statistics (NBS). 2015. *Monitoring Report of Poverty in Rural China* (中国农村贫困监测报告). Beijing: China Statistics Press.

National Bureau of Statistics (NBS). 2016. "Tabulation on the 2010 Population Census of China." Retrieved from: www.stats.gov.cn/tjsj/pcsj/rkpc/6rp/indexch.htm.

National Bureau of Statistics (NBS). 2018. "Population of Rural Poor People Has Decreased Significantly and the Income of Rural Residents in Poverty-Stricken Areas Has Increased Rapidly in 2017 (2017年全国农村贫困人口明显减少 贫困地区农村居民收入加快增长)." Stats. Gov.cn. February 1, 2018. Retrieved from: www.stats.gov.cn/tjsj/zxfb/201802/t20180201_1579703.html.

NBS, UNICEF China, and UNFPA China. 2017. "Population Status of Children in China in 2015: Facts and Figures." Retrieved from: www.unicef.cn/en/uploadfile/2017/1009/20171009112814506.pdf.

New Citizen Program. (2014). "Report on Migrant Children in China (中国流动儿童数据报告, 2014)." Retrieved from: www.cssn.cn/dybg/gqdy_sh/201506/t20150626_2049659.shtml.

National Health and Family Planning Commission (NHFPC). 2015. "An Analytical Report of the Fifth National Health Services Survey, 2013 (2013年第五次国家卫生服务调查分析报告)." Retrieved from: www.nhfpc.gov.cn/ewebeditor/uploadfile/2016/10/20161026163512679.pdf.

Nie, Hongping Annie. 2008. *The Dilemma of the Moral Curriculum in a Chinese Secondary School.* Lanham, Maryland: University Press of America.

Osborne, Cynthia, Lawrence M. Berger, and Katherine Magnuson. 2012. "Family Structure Transitions and Changes in Maternal Resources and Well-Being." *Demography* 49 (1): 23–47.

Pan, Lu, and Jingzhong Ye. 2014. "Pay Attention to the Education of Left-behind Children—Children of the Great Development: Education and Developmental Challenges of Rural Left-behind Children (关注留守儿童教育——

'大发展的孩子们': 农村留守儿童的教育与成长困境)." *Peking University Education Review* 3: 1–12.
Pearlin, Leonard I., and Carmi Schooler. 1978. "The Structure of Coping." *Journal of Health and Social Behavior* 19 (1): 2–21.
People's Daily. 2011. "Outline of the Twelfth Five Year Plan for National Economic and Social Development in the People's Republic of China (中华人民共和国国民经济和社会发展第十二个五年规划纲要)." March 17, 2011. Retrieved from: http://theory.people.com.cn/GB/14163131.html.
Perou, Ruth, Rebecca H. Bitsko, Stephen J. Blumberg, Patricia Pastor, Reem M. Ghandour, Joseph C. Gfroerer, Sarra L. Hedden, Alex E. Crosby, Susanna N. Visser, and Laura A. Schieve. 2013. "Mental Health Surveillance among Children—United States, 2005–2011." *MMWR Surveillance Summary* 62 (Suppl 2): 1–35.
Phillips, Deborah A., and Jack P. Shonkoff. 2000. *From Neurons to Neighborhoods: The Science of Early Childhood Development*. Washington, DC: National Academies Press.
Phillips, Tom. 2015. "Four 'Left-behind' Children in China Die of Poisoning after Being Abandoned." *The Guardian*, June 11, 2015, sec. World news. Retrieved from: www.theguardian.com/world/2015/jun/11/four-left-behind-children-in-china-die-of-poisoning-after-being-abandoned-by-parents.
Pittman, Laura D. 2007. "Grandmothers' Involvement among Young Adolescents Growing up in Poverty." *Journal of Research on Adolescence* 17 (1): 89–116.
Pittman, Laura D., and Michelle K. Boswell. 2007. "The Role of Grandmothers in the Lives of Preschoolers Growing Up in Urban Poverty." *Applied Developmental Science* 11 (1): 20–42.
Pong, Myra. 2014. *Educating the Children of Migrant Workers in Beijing: Migration, Education, and Policy in Urban China*. London and New York: Routledge.
Putnam, Robert B. 2015. *Our Kids: The American Dream in Crisis*. New York, NY: Simon and Schuster.
Pye, Lucian W. 1992. *The Spirit of Chinese Politics*. Cambridge, MA: Harvard University Press.
Qi, Di, and Yichao Wu. 2014. "Child Poverty in China – A Multidimensional Deprivation Approach." *Child Indicators Research* 7 (1): 89–118.
Qi, Xiaofei, and Edward C. Melhuish. 2017. "Early Childhood Education and Care in China: History, Current Trends and Challenges." *Early Years* 37 (3): 268–284.
Qi, Wei, Shenghe Liu, and Holan Jin. 2017. "Assessment of and Spatial Pattern of the Rate of Urbanization of the Hukou Population in China (中国户籍人口城镇化率的核算方法与分布格局)." *Geographical Research* 36 (4): 616–632.
Quoss, Bernita, and Wen Zhao. 1995. "Parenting Styles and Children's Satisfaction with Parenting in China and the United States." *Journal of Comparative Family Studies* 26 (2): 265–280.
Ren, Qiang, and Donald J. Treiman. 2016. "The Consequences of Parental Labor Migration in China for Children's Emotional Wellbeing." *Social Science Research* 58: 46–67.

Ren, Xuefei. 2013. *Urban China*. Cambridge: Polity Press.
Reynolds, Arthur J., Judy A. Temple, Suh-Ruu Ou, Irma A. Arteaga, and Barry A.B. White. 2011. "School-Based Early Childhood Education and Age-28 Well-Being: Effects by Timing, Dosage, and Subgroups." *Science* 333 (6040): 360–364.
Roberts, Kenneth. 1997. "China's 'Tidal Wave' of Migrant Labor: What Can We learn from Mexican Undocumented Migration to the United States?" *International Migration Review* 31: 247–293.
Rosenberg, Morris. 1979. *Conceiving the Self*. New York, NY: Basic Books.
Rosenzweig, Mark R., and Junsen Zhang. 2009a. "Do Population Control Policies Induce More Human Capital Investment? Twins, Birth Weight and China's 'One-Child' Policy." *The Review of Economic Studies* 76 (3): 1149–1174.
Rosenzweig, Mark R., and Junsen Zhang. 2009b. "Do Population Control Policies Induce More Human Capital Investment? Twins, Birth Weight and China's 'One-Child' Policy." *The Review of Economic Studies* 76 (3): 1149–1174. Retrieved from: https://doi.org/10.1111/j.1467-937X.2009.00563.x.
Luo, Renfu, Fang Jia, Ai Yue, Linxiu Zhang, Qijia Lyu, Yaojiang Shi, Meredith Yang, Alexis Medina, Sarah Kotb, and Scott Rozelle. 2017. "Passive Parenting and Its Association with Early Child Development." *Early Child Development and Care*, DOI: 10.1080/03004430.2017.1407318.
Sampson, Robert J. 2003. "The Neighborhood Context of Well-Being." *Perspectives in Biology and Medicine* 46 (3): S53–S64.
Schwarzer, Ralf, and A. Luszczynska. 2005. "Social Cognitive Theory." *Predicting Health Behaviour* 2: 127–169.
Shonkoff, Jack P., and Deborah A. Phillips, eds. 2000. *From Neurons to Neighborhoods: the Science of Early Childhood Development*. Washington, DC: National Academy Press.
Smith, Gregory C., and Patrick A. Palmieri. 2007. "Risk of Psychological Difficulties among Children Raised by Custodial Grandparents." *Psychiatric Services* 58 (10): 1303–1310.
Solinger, Dorothy. 1999. *Contesting Citizenship in Urban China: Peasant Migrants, the State, and the Logic of the Market*. Berkeley, CA: University of California Press.
Song, Yang. 2014. "What Should Economists Know about the Current Chinese Hukou System?" *China Economic Review* 29: 200–212.
Stata Corp. 2013. *Stata Survey Data Reference Manual, Release 13*. College Station, TX: Stata Corp LP.
State Council. 2011. "Outline of National Program for Child Development in China (2011–2020) (中国儿童发展纲要2011–2020)". Retrieved from: www.gov.cn/gongbao/content/2011/content_1927200.htm.
State Council. 2012. "Statements on Promoting the Balanced Development of Compulsory Education (国务院关于深入推进义务教育均衡发展的意见)."
State Council. 2014. "State Council Circular on Adjusting the Standards for Categorizing City Size (国务院关于调整城市规模划分标准的通知)." Gov.

cn. November 20, 2014. Retrieved from: www.gov.cn/zhengce/content/2014-11/20/content_9225.htm.

State Council. 2016a. "Several Statements on Promoting the Integrated Reform and Development of Urban- Rural Compulsory Education within Counties (关于统筹推进县域内城乡义务教育一体化改革发展的若干意见)."

State Council. 2016b. "Statements on Strengthening the Work of Caring for and Protection of Rural Left-behind Children (国务院关于加强农村留守儿童关爱保护工作的意见)."

State Council. 2016c. "Statements on Strengthening the Work of Protecting Children in Difficult Circumstances (国务院关于加强困境儿童保障工作的意见)."

State Council. 2016d. "State Council Circular on Disseminating the 13th Five-Year Plan for Poverty Alleviation (国务院关于印发'十三五'脱贫攻坚规划的通知)." Gov.cn. November 23, 2016. Retrieved from: www.gov.cn/gongbao/content/2016/content_5148746.htm.

State Council. 2018. "State Council Statement on Implementing the Lifelong Vocational Skills Training System (国务院关于推行终身职业技能培训制度的意见)." Gov.cn. May 8, 2018. Retrieved from: www.gov.cn/zhengce/content/2018-05/08/content_5289157.htm.

Sun, Yan. 1991. "The Chinese Protests of 1989: the Issue of Corruption." *Asian Survey* 31 (8): 762–782.

Tan, Charlene. 2017. "Chinese Responses to Shanghai's Performance in PISA." *Comparative Education* 53 (2): 209–223.

Tan, Ling, Tiansheng Xia, and Christy Reece. 2018. "Social and Individual Risk Factors for Suicide Ideation among Chinese Children and Adolescents: A Multilevel Analysis." *International Journal of Psychology* 53(2): 117–125.

Tang, Fang, and Ping Qin. 2015. "Influence of Personal Social Network and Coping Skills on Risk for Suicidal Ideation in Chinese University Students." *PLoS One* 10(3): e0121023.

Tang, Wen, Yi Mu, Xiaohong Li, Yanping Wang, et al. 2017 "Low Birthweight in China: Evidence from 441 Health Facilities between 2012 and 2014." *The Journal of Maternal-Fetal and Neonatal Medicine* 30 (16): 1997–2002.

Tang, Wenfang, and Benjamin Darr. 2012. "Chinese Nationalism and its Political and Social Origins." *Journal of Contemporary China* 21 (77): 811–826. DOI: 10.1080/10670564.2012.684965.

Tao, Qing, and Junyong Lu. 2011. "Rural Small Class Teaching, the Effective Ways to Promote the Balanced Development of the Urban and Rural Education." *Theory and Practice of Education* 34 (10): 24–6.

Thapar, Anita, Stephan Collishaw, Daniel S. Pine, and Ajay K. Thapar. 2012. "Depression in Adolescence." *The Lancet* 379 (9820): 1056–1067.

The Division of Migrant Population, National Health and Family Planning Commission. 2015. *China Migrant Population Development Report 2015*. China Population Press.

The Economist. 2015. "Pity the Children: China's Left-behind Generation." October 17, 2015.

The State Council Leading Group Office of Poverty Alleviation and Development. 2007. "Circular on Disseminating 'The Statement on the Implementation of the Rain and Dew Program in Poor Areas' and 'Guidance on the Implementation of Training on the Transfer of Poverty-Stricken Young and Middle-Aged Laborers' (关于印发《关于在贫困地区实施'雨露计划'的意见》和《贫困青壮年劳动力转移培训工作实施指导意见》的通知)." Gov.cn. March 30, 2007. Retrieved from: www.gov.cn/zwgk/2007-03/30/content_566578.htm.

Thomson, Elizabeth, Thomas L. Hanson, and Sara S. McLanahan. 1994. "Family Structure and Child Well-Being: Economic Resources vs. Parental Behaviors." *Social Forces* 73 (1): 221–242.

Tsang, Mun C., and Yanqing Ding. 2005. "Resource Utilization and Disparities in Compulsory Education in China." *China Review* 2005: 1–31.

Tsui, Ming, and Lynne Rich. 2002. "The Only Child and Educational Opportunity for Girls in Urban China." *Gender and Society* 16 (1): 74–92.

UNICEF, and WHO. 2004. *Low Birthweight: Country, Regional and Global Estimates*. UNICEF, New York, 2004. Retrieved from: www.unicef.org/publications/files/low_birthweight_from_EY.pdf.

UNICEF. 2014. *Children in China: An Atlas of Social Indicators, 2014*. (中国儿童发展指标图集 2014). Retrieved from: www.unicef.cn/en/atlas.

Waite, Linda J. 1995. "Does Marriage Matter?" *Demography* 32 (4): 483–507.

Waldfogel, Jane, Terry-Ann Craigie, and Jeanne Brooks-Gunn. 2010. "Fragile Families and Child Wellbeing." *The Future of Children/Center for the Future of Children, the David and Lucile Packard Foundation* 20 (2): 87.

Walker, Susan P., Theodore D. Wachs, Sally Grantham-McGregor, Maureen M. Black, Charles A. Nelson, Sandra L. Huffman, Helen Baker-Henningham, Susan M. Chang, Jena D. Hamadani, and Betsy Lozoff. 2011. "Inequality in Early Childhood: Risk and Protective Factors for Early Child Development." *The Lancet* 378 (9799): 1325–1338.

Wan, Minggang. 2009. "In the Name of Educational Equality and Balanced Development: The Potential Problems of School Consolidation in Rural China (以促进教育公平和教育均衡的名义：我国农村撤点并校带来的隐忧)." *Educational Research* 10: 19–20.

Wang, Fei-Ling. 2005. *Organizing Through Division and Exclusion: China's Hukou System*. Stanford University Press. Retrieved from: www.sup.org/books/title/?id=7081.

Wang, Fei-Ling. 2010. "Renovating the Great Floodgate: the Reform of China's Hukou System." In *One Country, Two Societies: Rural-Urban Inequality in Contemporary China*, edited by Martin K. Whyte, 335–366. Boston, MA: Harvard University Press.

Wang, Feng, Yong Cai, Ke Shen, and Stuart Gietel-Basten. 2018. "Is Demography Just a Numerical Exercise? Numbers, Politics, and Legacies of China's One-Child Policy." *Demography* 55 (2): 693–719.

Wang, Lei, Mengjie Li, Cody Abbey, and Scott Rozelle. 2018. "Human Capital and the Middle Income Trap: How Many of China's Youth Are Going to High School?" *The Developing Economies* 56 (2): 82–103.

Wang, Lamei, and Judi Mesman. 2015. "Child Development in the Face of Rural-to-Urban Migration in China: A Meta-Analytic Review." *Perspectives on Psychological Science* 10 (6): 813–831.

Wang, Qian, and Lei Chang. 2010. "Parenting and Child Socialization in Contemporary China," in *Oxford Handbook of Chinese Psychology*, ed. Michael Harris Bond. Oxford: Oxford University Press.

Wang, Qingbin, and Qin Zhou. 2010. "China's Divorce and Remarriage Rates: Trends and Regional Disparities." *Journal of Divorce and Remarriage* 51 (4): 257–267.

Wang, Ruiming, and Hong Zou. 2010. "Subjective Wellbeing of Migrant Children in Beijing (北京市流动儿童主观幸福感的特点)." *China Mental Health Journal* 24(2): 131–134.

Wang, Xin, Ang Zheng, Xin He, and Hanghang Jiang. 2014. "Integration of Rural and Urban Healthcare Insurance Schemes in China: an Empirical Research." *BMC Health Services Research* 14: 142. Retrieved from: https://doi.org/10.1186/1472-6963-14-142.

Wang, Xiong. 2011. "A Study on Excessive Large Class Sizes in Primary and Middle Schools of Our Country." In Yang, Dongping, and Chunqing Chai, eds. *Annual Report on China's Education 2011* (中国教育发展报告2011). Beijing, China: Social Sciences Academic Press.

Wei, Houkai, and Dali Yang. 1997. "Decentralization and Regional Educational Disparities in China(地方分权与中国地区教育差异)." *Social Sciences in China* 1997 (1): 98–113.

Weller, Elizabeth B., Angelica Kloos, Joon Kang, and Ronald A. Weller. 2006. "Depression in Children and Adolescents: Does Gender Make a Difference?" *Current Psychiatry Reports* 8 (2): 108–114.

Welzel, Christian, and Alejandro M. Alvarez. 2014. "Enlightening People: The Spark of Emancipative Values." In *The Civic Culture Transformed*, edited by Russell J. Dalton and Christian Welzel, 59–88. New York, NY: Cambridge University Press.

Wen, Jun, and Gu Chudan. 2017. "Urban-Rural Disparities in the Allocation of Basic Education Resources and Their Social Consequences (基础教育资源分配的城乡差异及其社会后果)." *School Bulletin of East China Normal University* 35 (2): 33–42.

Wen, Ming. 2008. "Family Structure and Children's Health and Behavior: Data From the 1999 National Survey of America's Families." *Journal of Family Issues* 29 (11): 1492–1519.

Wen, Ming, and Danhua Lin. 2012. "Child Development in Rural China: Children Left Behind by Their Migrant Parents and Children of Nonmigrant Families." *Child Development* 83 (1): 120–136. Retrieved from: https://doi.org/10.1111/j.1467-8624.2011.01698.x.

Wen, Ming, Shaobing Su, Xiaoming Li, and Danhua Lin. 2015. "Positive Youth Development in Rural China: The Role of Parental Migration." *Social Science and Medicine* 132: 261–269.

Whyte, Martin. 2010a. *Myth of the Social Volcano: Perceptions of Inequality and Distributive Injustice in Contemporary China*. Palo Alto, CA: Stanford University Press.

Whyte, Martin. 2010b. "The Paradoxes of Rural-Urban Inequality in Contemporary China." In *One Country, Two Societies: Rural-Urban*

Inequality in Contemporary China, edited by Martin K. Whyte, 1–28. Boston, MA: Harvard University Press.

World Bank. 2015. "China Overview." Retrieved from: www.worldbank.org/en/country/china/overview.

World Bank. 2017. "Labor Force Participation Rate, Female." Retrieved from: https://data.worldbank.org/indicator/SL.TLF.CACT.FE.ZS?locations=CN-US&year_high_desc=false.

Working Group of China Obesity Task Force (WGOC). 2004. "Body Mass Index Reference Norm for Screening Overweight and Obesity in Chinese Children and Adolescents." *China Journal of Epidemiology* 25 (2): 97–102.

Wu, Di, Shulun Huang, and Shaoyuan Chen. 2017. "More Migrant Children Are Returning: Where Is the Hometown of Those Living between Urban and Rural Areas? (流动儿童回流现增势 城乡夹心人何处是故乡)." *Caixin Media*. March 29, 2017. Retrieved from: http://china.caixin.com/2017-03-29/101071949.html.

Wu, Qiaobing, Deping Lu, and Mi Kang. 2015. "Social Capital and the Mental Health of Children in Rural China with Different Experiences of Parental Migration." *Social Science and Medicine* 132: 270–277.

Wu, Xiaolong Hugh, Dali L. Yang, and Lijun Chen. 2017. "The Politics of Quality-of-life Issues: Food Safety and Political Trust in China," *Journal of Contemporary China* 26 (106): 601–615.

Wu, Zhihui, and Jingmei Li. 2017. "Gaining Access to Urban Public Education for Children of Migrant Workers: Difficulties and Policy Choices (农民工随迁子女在城市接受义务教育的现实困境与政策选择)." *Educational Research* 9: 19–31.

Wu, Zhihui, and Yuyou Qin. 2017. *Rural Education Development in China: An Annual Report* (中国农村教育发展报告2017). Beijing: Beijing Normal University Publishing House.

Xi Jinping. 2017. "Secure a Decisive Victory in Building a Moderately Prosperous Society in All Respects and Strive for the Great Success of Socialism with Chinese Characteristics for a New Era." *China Daily*. November 4, 2017. Retrieved from: www.chinadaily.com.cn/china/19thcpcnationalcongress/2017-11/04/content_34115212.htm.

Xiang, Biao. 2007. "How Far Are the Left-behind Left behind? A Preliminary Study in Rural China." *Population, Space and Place* 13 (3): 179–191.

Xie, Yu. 2013. *Gender and Family in Contemporary China*. Research Report, Ann Arbor: Population Studies Center, University of Michigan Institute for Social Research. Retrieved from: www.psc.isr.umich.edu/pubs/pdf/rr13-808.pdf.

Xie, Yu, and Jingwei Hu. 2014. "An Introduction to the China Family Panel Studies (CFPS)." *Chinese Sociological Review* 47 (1): 3–29.

Xie, Yu, Zeqi Qiu, and Ping Lu. 2012. "China Family Panel Studies: Sample Design for the 2010 Baseline Survey." In *Technical Report Series: CFPS-1* (中国家庭追踪调查技术报告系列 (CFPS-1)). Institute of Social Science Survey, Peking University.

Xie, Yu, and Xiang Zhou. 2014. "Income Inequality in Today's China." *Proceedings of the National Academy of Sciences (PNAS)* 111 (19): 6928–6933.

Xinhua Net. 2010. "Outline of the National Medium- and Long-Term Plan for Education Reform and Development (2010–2020) (国家中长期教育改革和发展规划纲要 (2010–2020年))." July 29, 2010. Retrieved from: www.gov.cn/jrzg/2010-07/29/content_1667143.htm.

Xinhua Net. 2015. "How Hard Is It to Gain the Hukou in a Big City? Tracking the Hukou Policies in Beijing, Shanghai, Guangzhou, and Shenzhen (落户大城市到底有多难? 北上广深积分落户政策追踪)." Xinhua Net. December 13, 2015. Retrieved from: www.xinhuanet.com/politics/2015-12/13/c_1117443864.htm.

Xinhua Net. 2016. "Outline of the Thirteenth Five-Year Plan for National Economic and Social Development of the People's Republic of China (中华人民共和国国民经济和社会发展第十三个五年规划纲要)." Gov.cn. March 17, 2016. Retrieved from: www.gov.cn/xinwen/2016-03/17/content_5054992.htm.

Xinhua Net. 2017. "President Xi Delivers New Year Speech Vowing Resolute Reform in 2018." Xinhua Net. December 31, 2017. Retrieved from: www.xinhuanet.com/english/2017-12/31/c_136863397.htm.

Xiong, Chunwen. 2009. "New Trends in China's Rural Education since the Late 1990s (20世纪90年代末以来中国乡村教育的新趋势)." *Sociological Studies* 5: 110–140.

Xu, Anqi, and Yan Xia. 2014. "The Changes in Mainland Chinese Families during the Social Transition: A Critical Analysis." *Journal of Comparative Family Studies* 45 (1): 31–53.

Xu, Ying, Bo-sin Tang, and Edwin H.W. Chan. 2011. "State-led Land Requisition and Transformation of Rural Villages in Transitional China." *Habitat International* 35 (1): 57–65.

Xu, Guoying. 2013. "Analysis of the Value of the School Closure and Consolidation Policy of Rural Primary and Secondary Schools (农村中小学撤点并校政策价值分析)." *Theory and Practice of Education* 32 (31): 21–24.

Yang, Dali L. 1996. *Beyond Beijing: Liberalization and the Regions in China*. New York: Routledge.

Yang, Dali L. 2017a. "China's Illiberal Regulatory State in Comparative Perspective." *Chinese Political Science Review* 2 (1): 114–133.

Yang, Dali L. 2017b. "China's Troubled Quest for Order: Leadership, Organization and the Contradictions of the Stability Maintenance Regime." *Journal of Contemporary China* 26 (103): 35–53.

Yang, Guobin. 2016. "Heroic Fans of Nationalism." *Chinese Journal of Journalism and Communication* 11 (38): 25–32.

Yang, Lili, Zhihan Yan, Yuchuan Fu, Meimei Du, and Su Lui. 2015. "Parental Absence Affects Brain Development in Children." In *Radiological Society of North America*. Retrieved from: www.sciencedaily.com/releases/2015/11/151130084008.htm.

Yang, Mayfair Mei-hui. 1994. *Gifts, Favors, and Banquets: The Art of Social Relationships in China*. Ithaca, NY: Cornell University Press.

Yang, Yuan. 2018. "The Quiet Revolution: China's Millennial Backlash." *Financial Times*, April 17, 2018. www.ft.com/content/dae2c548-4226-11e8-93cf-67ac3a6482fd.

Ye, Jingzhong, Chunyu Wang, Huifang Wu, Congzhi He, and Juan Liu. 2013. "Internal Migration and Left-behind Populations in China." *Journal of Peasant Studies* 40 (6): 1119–1146.

Yeung, W. Jean, Miriam R. Linver, and Jeanne Brooks–Gunn. 2002. "How Money Matters for Young Children's Development: Parental Investment and Family Processes." *Child Development* 73 (6): 1861–1879.

Yi, Hongmei, Linxiu Zhang, Renfu Luo, Yaojiang Shi, Di Mo, Xinxin Chen, Carl Brinton, and Scott Rozelle. 2012. "Dropping Out: Why Are Students Leaving Junior High in China's Poor Rural Areas?" *International Journal of Educational Development* 32 (4): 555–563.

Yi, Hongmei, Linxiu Zhang, Yezhou Yao, Aiqin Wang, Yue Ma, Yaojiang Shi, James Chu, Prashant Loyalka, and Scott Rozelle. 2015. "Exploring the Dropout Rates and Causes of Dropout in Upper-Secondary Technical and Vocational Education and Training (TVET) Schools in China." *International Journal of Educational Development* 42: 115–23.

Yin, Shuai. 2008. "Exploratory Analysis of Rural and Urban Disparities in Medical Care and Health (我国城乡居民医疗健康差距探悉)." *Northern Economy* 190 (17): 32–34.

Yiu, Lisa, and Luo Yun. 2017. "China's Rural Education: Chinese Migrant Children and Left-behind Children." *Chinese Education and Society* 50: 207–314.

Yu, Shaoxiang. 2009. "NRCMS: A Big Feast? Or Chicken Bones? A Research Report on the Development of 'New Rural Cooperative Medical System' (新农合：是大餐？还是鸡肋？新农村合作医疗发展研究报告)." Retrieved from: www.iolaw.org.cn/showNews.asp?id=22842.

Yue, Ai, Yaojiang Shi, Renfu Luo, Jamie Chen, James Garth, Jimmy Zhang, Alexis Medina, Sarah Kotb, and Scott Rozelle. 2017. "China's Invisible Crisis: Cognitive Delays among Rural Toddlers and the Absence of Modern Parenting." *The China Journal* 78: 50–81.

Yuan, Ling. 2017. *The Green Moss Will Not Disappear* (青苔不会消失). Beijing: CITIC Press Corporation.

Zhang, Chong, Xueyi Wang, and Dan Zhang. 2014. "Urbanization, Unemployment Rate and China's Rising Divorce Rate." *Chinese Journal of Population Resources and Environment* 12 (2): 157–164.

Zhang, Fan, Qin Liu, Yong Zhao, Minhong Sun, and Hong Wang. 2011. "A Systematic Review of Studies on the Mental Health Issues of Left-behind Children in Our Country (我国留守儿童心理健康问题研究的系统评价)." *Chinese Journal of Evidence-based Medicine*, 2011 (8): 849–857.

Zhang, Guo, and Yongming Zeng. 2013. "The Rural-Urban Divide, Rural-Urban Integration, and Rural Population Development (城乡分割、城乡一体与农村人口发展)." *Journal of Sichuan Normal University (Social Sciences Edition)* 40 (6): 80–87.

Zhang, Qian, Xiaoyan Tan, Lianlong Yu, Huajin Qi, Xiaolong Yu, and Lingzhong Xu. 2013. "A Study of Overweight and Obesity Problems Among School-aged Children in Cities in Shandong and Influence Factors (山东省城市学龄儿童超重、肥胖现状及影响因素研究)." *Chinese Journal of Child Health Care* 5: 528–531.

Zhang, Tiedao, and Minxia Zhao. 2006. "Universalizing Nine-Year Compulsory Education for Poverty Reduction in Rural China." *International Review of Education* 52 (3): 261–286.

Zhang, Weiyuan, Yuyu Qin, and Junrui Wu. 2010. "An Analysis of Behavioral Problems Based on a Sample of 526 Migrant Children in Nanning City (南宁市536名流动儿童行为问题分析)." *Chinese Journal of School Health* 1: 60–61.

Zhang, Yingxiu, Zhaoxia Wang, Jinshan Zhao, and Zunhua Chu. 2016. "Prevalence of Overweight and Obesity among Children and Adolescents in Shandong, China: Urban-Rural Disparity." *Journal of Tropical Pediatrics* 62 (4): 293–300. Retrieved from: www.ncbi.nlm.nih.gov/pubmed/26966244.

Zhao, Dan, and Bruno Parolin. 2011. "School Mapping Restructure in China: What Role for the Small Rural School?" *Frontiers of Education in China* 6 (2): 248–278. Retrieved from: https://doi.org/10.1007/s11516-011-0131-5.

Zhao, Suisheng. 2013. "Foreign Policy Implications of Chinese Nationalism Revisited: The Strident Turn." *Journal of Contemporary China* 22 (82): 535–553.

Zhao, Suisheng, ed. 2014. *Construction of Chinese Nationalism in the Early 21st Century: Domestic Sources and International implications*. New York, NY: Routledge.

Zhao, Xinle. 2016. "Report on National Media Commemorating the Long March (全国媒体纪念长征报道)." *People.cn*, October 25, 2016. Retrieved from: http://media.people.com.cn/n1/2016/1025/c40606-28804286.html.

Zhao, Zhen, and Zhihui Wu. 2015. "The Rural Cultural Crisis Brought about by School Closure and Consolidation (撤点并校带来的乡村文化危机)." *Modern Primary and Secondary Education* 31 (1): 11–15.

Zheng, Lei, and Yingxiong Wu. 2014. "Impact of Labor Migration on the Educational Development of Left-behind Children: Evidence from Western Rural Areas (劳动力迁移对农村留守儿童教育发展的影响——来自西部农村地区调查的证据)." *Journal of Beijing Normal University (Social Science)* 2: 139–145.

Zhou, Chengchao, Sean Sylvia, Linxiu Zhang, Renfu Luo, Hongmei Yi, Chengfang Liu, Yaojiang Shi, Prashant Loyalka, James Chu, and Alexis Medina. 2015. "China's Left-behind Children: Impact of Parental Migration on Health, Nutrition, and Educational Outcomes." *Health Affairs* 34 (11): 1964–1971.

Zhou, Mi, Guangsheng Zhang, Scott Rozelle, Kaleigh Kenny, and Hao Xue. 2018. "Depressive Symptoms of Chinese Children: Prevalence and Correlated Factors among Subgroups." *International Journal of Environmental Research and Public Health* 15 (2): 283.

Zhou, Minhui, Rachel Murphy, and Ran Tao. 2014. "Effects of Parents' Migration on the Education of Children Left behind in Rural China." *Population and Development Review* 40 (2): 273–292.

Zhou, Shu, and Monit Cheung. 2017. "Hukou System Effects on Migrant Children's Education in China: Learning from Past Disparities." *International Social Work* 60 (6): 1327–1342. Retrieved from: https://doi.org/10.1177/0020872817725134.

Zhou, Xueguang. 2004. *The State and Life Chances in Urban China: Redistribution and Stratification, 1949–1994*. Cambridge, UK: Cambridge University Press.

Zhuo, Lang, Gu Yuming, et al. 2007. "Multi-factor Analysis of the Participation Rate in the New Cooperative Medical System in Jiangsu Province (江苏省新型农村合作医疗参合率多因素分析)." *China Rural Health Service Administration* 27 (11): 810–811.

Zong, Xin-Nan, and Li, Hui. 2014. "Physical Growth of Children and Adolescents in China over the Past 35 Years." *Bulletin of the World Health Organization* 92 (8): 555–564. Retrieved from: http://doi.org/10.2471/BLT.13.126243.

Zou, Hong, Zhiyong Qu, and Qiuling Zhang. 2005. "A Survey of Migrant Children's Development and Needs in Nine Cities of China (中国九城市流动儿童发展与需求调查)." *Youth Studies* 2: 1–7.

Index

academic performance 55–56, 59, 61, 73, 97, 102
adult supervision 3
adolescents 4, 41, 44, 59, 99, 112, 117–118, 122, 127
affectionate interaction 71
agricultural resident 14
anti-poverty drive 125
anti-poverty programs 129
authoritarian leadership 78
authority relations 79, 83

basic public health care 24
bare-foot doctors 24
Beijing 15, 71, 92, 128
birth planning 1, 19, 25
body mass index (BMI) 33, 35
brain development 99

caregiver encouragement 118
caregiver-child relationship 5
childcare 5, 125
child obesity 36, 39
childhood sickness 103–104
China Family Panel Studies (CFPS) 5–7, 9, 12, 13n4, 13n6, 26–28, 33–35, 40n2, 41–43, 48n2, 48n4–6, 49, 53, 56, 64, 66–68, 71, 73, 75n1, 78–89, 91–97, 103, 108, 112, 120, 127
Confucian tradition 63
cognitive capability 63
community 4–6, 22, 39n2, 63–64, 66, 75, 86, 102, 121, 129; rural 5, 24, 26, 30, 31, 65, 75, 121, 129; urban 5, 6, 45, 64, 125

compulsory education age 51
compulsory formal schooling 62n1
college aspirations 50–53, 61, 102
Cultural Revolution 19, 24

de-collectivization 15
demographic structure 21
developmental deficits 3
depression 3, 12, 41, 44, 99, 102
despotic authority 78
disparities 21, 23, 101, 120, 128; developmental 3–4; economic 2; regional 26; rural-urban 2, 5, 7–8, 27, 32, 42–43, 74–75, 103, 112
drop-out rates 22, 61

economic boom 77, 120
economic well-being 12, 26–32, 104
educational access 17
educational attainment 12, 49, 61, 112, 117–118, 122
educational barriers 17
education status 59, **60**, 118
emigration 21, 101–102
emotional deficits 48
emotional difficulties 17
ethnicity **7, 92**, 103–104, 112
exclusionary policies 3, 90, 121

familial hierarchy 78, 88
family circumstances 9, 86
family configurations 8
family functioning 5, 48, 63
family involvement 68
family planning policy 2, 12, 18

Index

family structure 5, 37, 47–48, 67, 91, 101
floating population 15

gender dynamics 83
gender imbalances 19
gender roles 81–83, 91
generational differences 81–82
government aid 27, **28–29**, 31, 121
Great Leap Forward 14, 24

happiness 4, 41–43, 45, 102–103, 105, 108–112, 118, 121–122
Heckman, J. 12n1
health insurance coverage 33, 35, 121
high school attendance 61
home environment 5, 63–64, 67–68, 75, 122, 126, 129
house crowding 27–31
hukou **7**, 9, 13n7, 14, 51, 53, 62n2, 67, **92**, 100n1, 121, 123, 127–129
human trafficking 18

imbalanced growth 67
inadequate parenting 98, 125
income gaps: between rich and poor in China 32; between urban and rural areas 2
individual autonomy 78
industrialization 2, 15–16, 90
infant mortality 4, 24, 33
institutional arrangements 14
institutionalized disadvantages 101
institutionalized inequalities 123
intact families 30, 39, 45–47, 52–57, 60–61, 66–68, 71–73, 99, 101–103, 109, 112, 117

job market 59; segmented 100

left-behind children 3–4, 12, 13n3, 13n8, 17–18, 30, 37–39, 41, 45, 47, 52–53, 56–58, 61, 62n3, 66–68, 71–75, 90–94, 97–103, 108–109, 120–121, 123, 126–128; broad and narrow definitions of 9
life expectancy 19, 24
life functioning 47
living arrangements 4, 8–9, 27–**31**, 37–**38**, 42, 45, **47**, 52–53, 56–57, 60, 66, 70–72, 91, *95*, **99**, 103, 108, 112; income insecurity 125; information gap 86
low birthweight 12, 33–39, 105, 121
"low-end population" 128

Mao era 19, 24, 73
malnutrition 26, 34, 37, 125
marital dissolution 48, 67, 101
massive migration 16, 90
material deprivation 26, 71
megacities 128
migrant children 3, 30, 38–39, 45–47, 53, 57–**58**, 61, 62n3, 67–68, 71, **92**, 121, 123, 126–129
migration 8, 45, 67, 90–103, 105, 119n1, 121–122, 127–128: internal 8, 18, 30, 48, 91, 100; patterns 93
migration point system (scheme) 25n1, 128
modernization theory 78
morbidity 37–38, 103, 105, 118, 122

National Bureau of Statistics (NBS) 2–4, 6–8, 13n3, 16–17, 19, 26, 32n2, 91, 128
National Program for Child Development (2011–2020) 1
neighborhood safety 5
New Urbanization Plan 127
"no tuition and no fee" 23
non-agricultural resident 14
nuclear and stem families 19; unbalanced economic growth 2

only children 2, 19, 105, 108
overcrowding: classroom 3

parental absence 3, 5, 8, 12, 48, 56, 67, 90, 91–105, **106**, 109, **110**, 112, 117–118, 119n1, 121–123, 126
parenting practices 4, 64, 72, 75, 118, 126
parenting styles 5, 64, 112
patrilineal values 81–82, 88
peer groups 4
personal relationships 48n6, 85
physical health problems 17
physical safety problems 18
physical soundness 35

physical well-being 2, 33, 103, 105
political culture 78
political upheavals 24, 86
Population Census 2
population urbanization regime 127–128
positive parenting behaviors 63, 71, 122
poverty 1–2, 5–6, 12, 24, 26, **27–28**, 30–34, 59, 71, 90, 104–05, 112, 121, 124–129
poverty alleviation 31, 75, 121, 123–125, 127; targeted 125
poverty line 26–27, 32n2, 124
pre-school education 50–51, 61, 125–127
psychological well-being 4, 41–43, 101, 105
psychological health 22, 41, 98, 103
psychological depression 42
Purchasing Power Parity exchange rate 32n2

"Rain and Dew Plan" 127
region 4, 7, 30, 39, 41, 67, 103–104; central 13n5, 30, 54, 61, 90, 93–97, 103; coastal 9, 90; eastern 13n5, 30, 61, 92–97, 103; less-developed 2; urban 4; western 13n5, 30, 54, 61, 90, 93–97, 104

sample design 5
school consolidation 3, 12, 21–22, 52–53, 66
school enrollment 4, 21, 49, 50–54, 59, 61
schooling interruption 116
schools 4, 5, 19, 49, 63–64; central 21–23; elementary 49; high 58–59, 62n3, 127; middle 22, 53, 69; pre- 49, 69; primary 19, 21–22, 53, 66, 69; private 15; public 17, 62n3, 122, 126, 129; rural 21, 61, 62n3, 69, 129; urban 53, 69; village 22
self-efficacy 42

self-esteem 3, 4, 12, 17, 41–48
service capacity 124
sex ratio at birth (SRB) 19
sexual harassment 18
Shanghai 15, 92, 128
social inequality 78, 83–84
social norms 5
social service 2, 5, 9, 15, 63–64
social stigma 73
social well-being 4, 12, 41–48
societal unfairness 83
socioeconomic status 5
spousal relationship 5
State Council 1, 9, 22, 33, 54, 91, 124–127, 145–147; Alleviation and Development 127; Leading Group Office of Poverty 125; Legal Affairs Office 15, General Office of 125–126, 136
structural inequalities 90, 122–123
subjective well-being 99, 109, 118
sub-par educational achievement 18
subsistence farming 90

teaching quality 5, 21, 23, 56, 59
temporary urban resident permits 15
"Two Exemptions and One Subsidy" 126

UNICEF 13n2, 24, 27, 33, 91, 125
United Nations Convention on the Rights of the Child 1
upward mobility 83, 86
urban bias 14
urban intact families 30, 47, 52–53, 57, 60–61, 66–67, 71–72
Urban Resident Committee 6
urbanization 2, 12, 16, 18, 90–91, 121, 127–129

Villager's Committee 6
vulnerable children 2, 3, 5, 41, 48, 112, 124–125, 129

youthful optimism 84